Off the Hook

"In *Off the Hook*, Timothy O'Malley confronts squarely the seamy reality of the hookup culture. He offers alternative pathways filled with appreciation for God-given sexuality, well lived in unselfish, faithful, and joyous love. This book provides a treasure trove for all affected by the hookup culture and those who minister to them."

Most Rev. Joseph E. Kurtz
Archbishop of Louisville

"The realities of today's hook-up culture are as undeniable as they are destructive. Timothy O'Malley sees the sacrament of marriage as a remedy to this sickness of self-serving romance. *Off the Hook* helps us dive into the marital vocation, which calls us to follow Christ's example of self-giving love for the sake of the other. Whether you are twenty-five years married or discerning the vocation, this book will help you love more deeply and lead to a richer understanding of how marriage sanctifies a couple—and, in turn, the culture."

Jason A. Kidd
Marriage and Family Director
Archdiocese of Portland in Oregon

"Experience is an important teacher for most of us, shaping what we do and who we become. Today, young adults are taught important lessons about sex, love, and relationships by the hookup culture. But these lessons are false. As Timothy O'Malley explains in *Off the Hook*, the practices learned from hookup culture encourage young people to become more self-centered, more anxious, and more alienated from genuine love. Thankfully, in this important book O'Malley points young adults and those who guide them to better practices and to an identity that is much more likely to lead them to genuine love."

W. Bradford Wilcox
Director of the National Marriage Project
University of Virginia

"*Off the Hook* takes a raw and eye-opening look at the current state of dating and marriage in our world and shows how the beauty, goodness, and truth of the Church's teachings provide the answers to what we are really looking for. Tim O'Malley authentically proclaims a stunning and hopeful message—the Church has the answer to what ails us."

Kevin and Lisa Cotter
Former FOCUS missionaries and coauthors of *Dating Detox*

"It's rare to find a book that mentions a booty call alongside the thoughts of von Hildebrand, among other theologians. Timothy O'Malley manages to explain the seriousness of today's hookup culture while never abandoning the hope of the nuptial mystery. With down-to-earth language and practical reflection exercises for anyone's vocational journey, *Off the Hook* needs to be on your reading list!"

Michael St. Pierre
Executive Director
Catholic Campus Ministry Association

What University of Notre Dame students are saying about *Off the Hook*

"This book revolutionized the way I imagine my future, and it has been incredibly edifying for my family life today. Professor O'Malley's work is clear, engaging, and full of beauty. He left me wholly convinced that the sacramentality of Christian marriage is underappreciated even among Catholics, and he has given me the tools to articulate to my own family and friends what we believe about married life signing God's love in the world."

Maureen Schweninger
Class of 2019

"Professor Timothy O'Malley offers a rare blend of shrewd insight and practical wisdom on marriage, invaluable for persons of any age or vocation. As a young Catholic, I love how he is able to articulate the beauty of marriage and its meaning as a sacrament in ways that are profoundly relevant to me. He has an uncanny ability to concretize lofty theology into something accessible for the average person."

Michael Singleton
Class of 2018

"Professor O'Malley shows a deep understanding of his students' lives, engaging us with compassion and humor. Refreshingly frank, O'Malley seamlessly integrates rigorous theology with personal testimony and critical research to provide a clear and accessible answer to our confusion and longing. O'Malley's countercultural insights not only provoke me to examine the way I live, but invite me to enter into a more fulfilling way to love. His class was life changing and this book is too. I can't recommend it enough!"

Sofia Carozza
Class of 2019

"Powerful and wonderfully real, *Off the Hook* honestly and personally relays the reality of love in a way that challenges us to recommit, renew, and reconceive our relationships with our loved ones, families, the world, and above all with God. This is a beautiful and extraordinary book."

Katherine Sisk
Class of 2018

"Tired of a culture that cheapens sexuality? Seeking a new story? Search no further. Timothy O'Malley presents the alluring mystery of a sacrament that heals and enables true freedom to love. The radical witness of marriage is precisely the couple's daily commitment to be a lasting sign of God's love in the world."

Grace Mariette Agolia
Class of 2017
Boston College School of Theology and Ministry Class of 2019

Off the Hook

God, Love, Dating, and Marriage in a Hookup World

Timothy P. O'Malley

McGrath Institute for Church Life
University of Notre Dame

Ave Maria Press · AVE · Notre Dame, Indiana

_____

© 2018 by Timothy P. O'Malley

All rights reserved. No part of this book may be used or reproduced in any manner whatsoever, except in the case of reprints in the context of reviews, without written permission from Ave Maria Press®, Inc., P.O. Box 428, Notre Dame, IN 46556, 1-800-282-1865.

Founded in 1865, Ave Maria Press is a ministry of the United States Province of Holy Cross.

www.avemariapress.com

Paperback: ISBN-13 978-1-59471-821-2

E-book: ISBN-13 978-1-59471-822-9

Cover image © Heather Landis.

Cover and text design by Samantha Watson.

Printed and bound in the United States of America.

Library of Congress Cataloging-in-Publication Data is available.

To Kara O'Malley, my beloved spouse,
whose friendship has led me into the mystery
of the kingdom of God.

To students of my Nuptial Mystery course
whose questions and insights made this work possible.

Contents

Introduction

The Sacrament of Marriage is a healing and sanctifying medicine. This claim had not occurred to me when I approached the altar with my wife-to-be on December 3, 2005. My inability to recognize the healing properties of marriage was not because my fiancée and I were unconcerned about the religious orientation of marriage. In fact the first task we checked off our engagement list was not assembling our wedding registry, discerning the right color scheme for wedding invitations, or finding the perfect cake for our reception. It was planning our wedding liturgy. We prayed over the reading options for our Mass. We pored over options for the Eucharistic Prayer and the Nuptial Blessing. We presented our preferences for these prayers to the priest around the same time we booked not one but two choirs for the wedding. Intending to marry during the season of Advent, we chose hymns in which the assembly could express their longing for the final coming of Jesus Christ. The centerpieces at our reception were Advent wreaths. While some couples engage in a battle with the parish musician to include a secular song at the wedding Mass, we lobbied for the Litany of the Saints (we lost).

But even with all our enthusiasm and careful preparation for our wedding liturgy, we did not imagine that the marriage rite we celebrated that day would provide a healing and sanctifying medicine for the rest of our lives. Like many young couples, we saw our wedding day as a single—albeit the most important— moment in a long line of adult accomplishments: earning a driver's license, getting into college, graduating, finding a career in which we could flourish, and then getting hitched. Ideally, other marks of adulthood—including the birth of children, purchasing our first home, and promotions at work (when we *finally* finished graduate school)—would follow after our nuptial union.

Things didn't work out quite the way we thought. The fairly easy upward mobility we had experienced as recent college graduates was interrupted when we moved to Boston during our first year of marriage. My wife's first job in youth ministry proved more challenging than she had imagined. I was disappointed in the quality of my graduate program and pondered whether pursuing a doctorate in theology might have been the craziest thing I'd ever done (other than hiking alone in a snake-infested field that one time). After years of experiencing the flourishing of our relationship in the company of friends, we were in a new city and alone for the first time. However, relying on the friendship we had established during our first months of marriage, we dealt with these problems in short order.

Then, a year or so after moving to Boston, after the turmoil in grad school and the loneliness had faded away, we decided it was time to have a kid. Six unsuccessful, although very fun, months later, we began to see fertility specialists. After a barrage of tests, we were diagnosed with "unexplained infertility." With this diagnosis, our easy story of upward mobility ended with a crash.

It wasn't that children were out of the picture. Conception was always a possibility, and so was adoption, something we did pursue (we are now the parents of two adopted children). Nonetheless, for the first time, we had to construct a new story for our lives. I found my restored story in a text from St. Paul that I had been contemplating in my studies:

> I urge you therefore, brothers, by the mercies of God, to offer your bodies as a living sacrifice, holy and pleasing to God, your spiritual worship. Do not conform yourselves to this age but be transformed by the renewal of your mind, that you may discern what is the will of God, what is good and pleasing and perfect. (Rom 12:1–2)

This exhortation—one of the options for the wedding liturgy that we didn't choose—was an epiphany for me. The story of upward mobility was a myth. Christian marriage was not one stop along the way in the pursuit of success. It was a sacrament that made it possible to offer one's very body as a sacrifice of love. Kara and I had conformed ourselves to the world, assuming that marriage would unfold as a "happily ever after" that was simply about us. Butting up against the trauma of infertility, we realized that our commitment to our marriage vows, our promise to love one another until the very end of our lives, wasn't about our individual fairy tale. Marriage was actually about the renewal of the world.

This moment of realization was not an occasion for naïve hope. The diagnosis of infertility stung. Yet as we contemplated the mystery of Christ's life, death, and resurrection at each Sunday Mass, we discovered that every aspect of our lives could be offered to God—the joyful and sorrowful moments alike. As I watched my spouse deal with the diagnosis of infertility, as she pushed us to consider foster care and adoption, as we endured our particular cross, our love deepened. Slowly, we began to see our story as planted within the saving narrative of God's redeeming love.

The Story of Hookup Culture

My wife and I were lucky; we enjoyed luxuries that allowed us to compose a new story for our lives, one grounded in the sacredness of Christian marriage. Our finances were in order, something rare for graduate students living in Boston. We lived together easily, a grace that has not been bestowed on every one of our friends. We had the support of our married parents and several mentor couples at our parish. But most importantly, we married young (relative to others of our generation), transitioning into adulthood with the support of a devoted spouse.

Most of the undergraduate students I teach at the University of Notre Dame will not be so lucky. While many of them will have a good deal more money than we had in the early days of our marriage (not a difficult accomplishment) and many will have the support of their parents and other couples, they won't marry in their early twenties. Instead, they'll be pulled into the plot lines of another story, a different one from the myth of upward mobility we had to deconstruct in the early years of our marriage. The narrative that will control their dating years, and form their understanding of the nature of love, is the hookup culture.

Hooking up is not new. When I was in college in the early aughts, we often spoke of hooking up, an ambiguous term that could mean anything from kissing someone in a drunken stupor on the dance floor to going home with them at the end of the night. Hookups were part of the drama of college life but were by no means normative. We thought of hookups as interruptions to regular dating practices such as attending dances and hanging out on the quad late into the night having life-altering conversations. And many hookups led to long-term relationships.

Today, the hookup remains ambiguous, but over the past fifteen years, it has become the principal means through which young adults meet, date, and (sometimes) marry. On a typical weekend in a city or in a college town, a typical young adult goes out and gets drunk. Drunkenness eliminates the last barrier to the hookup—the possibility of authentic communication. The young adult then has sex with someone. Perhaps the two meet up through a dating app like Tinder. Perhaps they've known each other for years and needed a bit of "liquid courage" to finally act. Often, among both men and women, there is romantic interest beneath the surface of the hookup, but in hookup world, everything begins with sex. According to the 2014 *Relationships in America* survey, 20 to 25 percent of men and women presently in a relationship (including marriage) had sex "'after we met, but before we began to consider ourselves as being in a relationship.'"[1] Donna Freitas, who has written about the hookup culture, concludes:

> For all intents and purposes, the hookup has replaced the first date on campus. When you encounter college couples today, chances are they got into their committed relationship through a serial hookup. This also means it is likely they had sex before they went out on a date or had a serious conversation about their feelings for each other. And it almost certainly means that the couple engaged in many drunken encounters before ever becoming sexually intimate while sober. In this culture, the sex comes first, then openness and communication, but only much, much later.[2]

Whether or not Freitas's claim is true of every relationship, the hookup has become part of the cultural script of young adult life. A cultural script is an unspoken story that guides how we act in the world. It functions in the background of our lives. For Freitas, the cure for the hookup culture is to invite college students to examine this script and to make reasonable decisions about the future of their sexual lives. Each student must construct an original, personal narrative about what constitutes "good sex," a term Freitas uses to refer to a meaningful sexual life. As she notes, good sex "could include hooking up, a long-term love, romance, dating, saving sex for a later date (be that next semester or for marriage), or taking a 'time-out' from sex for a while."[3]

I agree with Freitas that the hookup culture is a problem, one that requires a reasonable response from the academy, the Church, and society. Hookup culture is closely linked to sexual violence, pornography, and perhaps worst of all for the future of marriage an individualistic approach to love that makes commitment difficult. Those who have performed as actors in this cultural script will find it difficult to commit to a single person for the rest of their lives. They may opt out of marriage altogether.

But Freitas's account of hookup culture is naïve about the kind of medicine that is needed to heal this culture. Is it really as easy for us as Freitas suggests to reason our way to what constitutes "good sex" for us? After all, we learn to participate in a culture through our bodies first, not through reason. My son and daughter learn the culture of Christianity not through critical thinking and discussion around the dinner table but through the practices we perform around the home. It is these practices that stick with us for the rest of our lives. Even if someone has determined that "good sex" includes participating in hookups, that person does not escape the side effects of regularly hooking up. Hookup culture continues to write itself upon their bodies, forming them to separate the act of sex from loving communion.

Freitas is not alone in failing to recognize the formative quality of practice. Many of my students have argued in class that we can perform any action without consequence as long as we enter into it with the right attitude; they hold that the practice is a problem only if we misunderstand it. But that's not how practice works.

For example, during college I began to treat Friday as a day of leisure. On Thursday nights, I would go out to bars.

I would come home late, sleep in, and sometimes go to class. Homework was ignored. When I entered graduate school, I knew that Friday could no longer be a day of pure leisure. But the way my body was formed through specific habits took a lot longer to adjust than my reason. I no longer went out to bars on Thursday nights, but I did rise late on Friday mornings. I procrastinated, going for long walks rather than hitting the books. It wasn't until after graduate school, when I had a full-time job, that I began to participate in new practices and was healed of my Friday laziness.

Participation in hookup culture presents the same kind of problem; it tells us a story about love that forms our imaginations, even if we are not fully aware of it. The narrative hookup culture tells us that love and sex are for sale, easily purchased and then left behind when new options present themselves. It forms us to see a separation between love and sex, between communion with another person and the pleasure we experience during sex. Whether we are aware of it or not, this attitude becomes a part of how we imagine, and therefore approach, love and marriage.

Just as I had to take up new practices when I got a job at a university (thus breaking my Friday sloth), we need novel practices to replace the hookup culture and allow us to participate in a different culture—a culture in which love and sex are understood as part of the salvation of the human being. It is the argument of this book that the Catholic Sacrament of Marriage, particularly the wedding Mass itself, serves as a rich resource for developing these new practices. Sacramental practice, something that forms our very bodies, is needed to get us off the hook of the hookup culture.

A Counter Liturgy to Hookup Culture

To claim that the Catholic wedding liturgy could function as a balm for the hookup culture may seem a bit odd. The decline in sacramental marriages in the Catholic Church has been steep over the last twenty-five years. According to a leading compiler of Church statistics, in 1990, there were 55.7 million Catholics in the United States and 326,079 marriages. In 2017, there were 68.5 million Catholics and only 144,148 marriages.[4] Surely, there are better ways of responding to the hookup culture than focusing on a sacramental rite that many emerging adults do not participate in. Wouldn't it be better to host a Theology on Tap or other casual discussion about sex and the hookup culture?

In my work both as an academic and as a teacher, I have discovered that while many young adult Catholics may not be actively involved in the sacramental life of the Church, they are interested in the official liturgical prayer of the Church. On college campuses throughout the United States, I have seen significant numbers show up to hear my talks on the Rite of Marriage. My course at Notre Dame on the Sacrament of Marriage grew from sixty students in the fall of 2016 to 150 in the fall of 2017. When I gave a talk on how to date in the hookup culture, using the Sacrament of Marriage as the basis for the discussion, 170 undergraduates came out on a beautiful spring evening when even I didn't want to be there. At Michigan State University, eighty students showed up—while a basketball game was being played on campus—to hear about the Sacrament of Marriage.

These numbers are consistent with those reported by colleagues who teach about marriage. There is something about the marriage liturgy that draws the attention of students swimming in the sea of the hookup culture. It meets what Italian catechist and biblical theologian Sofia Cavalletti calls the "exigence of the students"—their deepest need to love and to be loved.[5] Young children delight in the parable of the Good Shepherd, discovering a God who will pursue them in love to the very ends of the earth. Young adults likewise discern in the Church's rites an image of Jesus as the Bridegroom who comes to transform human love into divine love.

This interest in the liturgical rites of the Church would not surprise Reformed Christian philosopher James K. A. Smith. Smith describes in his work how we as human beings are constantly formed by what he calls *cultural liturgies*. He would say that we are liturgical beings whether we want to be or not. These cultural liturgies, such as going to the shopping mall or remaining connected to the outside world through the iPhone, "shape and constitute our identities by forming our most fundamental desires and our most basic attunement to the world."[6] If the Church is to counteract the formation provided by these cultural liturgies, she will do so most effectively through her own liturgical practice.

The hookup culture is a cultural liturgy of sorts. Hooking up at a party or gazing upon the naked flesh in a porn video instills a certain narrative of dating, of marriage, and of family life within us. We are taught that commitment doesn't matter, that our partner's body is for our own sexual enjoyment, that the final purpose of sex is not procreation or communion but pleasure.

This is not the kind of story that leads to a happy ending. And it's also not the kind of story that young adults ultimately want to believe in. As Freitas concludes about the hookup culture, "Women and men both learn to shove their desires deep down into a dark place, to be revealed to no one. They learn to be ashamed if they long for love, and embarrassed if they fail to uphold the social contract of hookup culture."[7] Hookup culture does not just promote sexual sin. It forms how we understand love and thus what it means to be a human being.

What my students long for is love. They want to be able to fall in love with someone, to share their whole lives with another person without the expectation that they will be reduced to a sexual plaything. They want to get married and have kids. They want a happy home. They want communion—a love in which two human beings experience a union of wills, of desires, of day-to-day life—with one another.

And even if they're not aware of it, they want the most important thing of all. They want this love to be the source of their salvation, introducing them into the very life of God through the sacred normalness of married life. In studying the liturgical rite by which two people are joined in marriage, many of these young people learn, as Pope Francis reminds us, that "the sacrament [of marriage] is a gift given for the sanctification and salvation of the spouses."[8] They discover that they want to participate in the counter liturgy provided by the marriage rite of the Church.

A Nuptial Mystagogy

In what the Church calls a mystagogical approach to formation for marriage, *Off the Hook* contemplates the marriage as a medicine for the hookup culture. Mystagogy, as the *Catechism of the Catholic Church* explains, is an initiation into the mystery of Christ "by proceeding from the visible to the invisible, from the sign to the thing signified, from the 'sacraments' to the 'mysteries'" (*CCC*, 1075). In the Rite of Marriage, scripture is read. Vows are uttered. Rings are exchanged. Prayers are offered over the couple. The Eucharist is received. The couple is blessed.

Each of these moments has a meaning not reducible to the action itself. The Church's public prayer (her liturgy) points us to a form of life, a way of loving God and neighbor, that has the potential to renew the world. Every liturgy of the Church is meant to be a "lived liturgy in which each instant of life should become a 'moment' of grace."[9] We contemplate the Church's way of praying in order to remember anew those stories of salvation, those healing practices that restore us to "our vocation as creatures made in the image and likeness of God."[10]

The nuptial liturgy, in particular, is a rich source for this kind of reflection. While we participate week after week in the Eucharist, we are normally married only once, so it is easy to see the wedding as an isolated ceremony. But the wedding liturgy is more than this. It is meant to stick with us throughout our lives. The story of salvation that we hear in the scriptures—God's nuptial love for men and women—is meant to be the primary story through which we make sense of our own married love. The vows, or more formally the act of consent, create a bond between man and woman that endures unto death itself. Their consent consecrates the couple to become a living sacrifice of divine love for the whole world. The rings become signs of this permanent bond, an image of the very love of God. The Nuptial Blessing orders the couple's love to acts of radical hospitality, including becoming parents (God willing). The wedding ceremony ends, but the Sacrament of Marriage is permanent. To savor the nuptial mystery in the wedding liturgy is to delight in what God has accomplished among married couples.

This book treats each moment of the Catholic wedding liturgy, showing how it can be a healing balm for those suffering from the effects of hookup culture.

In chapter 1, I look at the cultural liturgy of the hookup, showing how this antiliturgy desecrates human love. It leads to an understanding of love grounded not in communion but in consuming the other either through sexual experience or pornography. The hookup culture avoids communication and communion. Many young people end up participating in this culture not because they like it, but out of fear. They're afraid to truly give themselves away in love.

In chapter 2, I provide a description of the natural order of love. "Falling in love" is a natural good. We know this. After all, you don't need to be a devout Christian to experience love. But knowing that people "fall in love" doesn't yet reveal to us the nature of love. Often, it's the most common experiences—like beauty, friendship, and suffering—that necessitate the deepest thinking. In this chapter, I explain love as a gift of self that is not reducible to feelings or desires. Love is a mutual gift between persons that leads to communion. True love is always an act of communication, and thus whatever the hookup culture is about, it's not about love.

In chapter 3, I turn to the story at the heart of the wedding liturgy as found in the scriptures. During the wedding, our love stories are taken up into the bigger narrative of God's love for the Church. We discover that we are created for communion with one another. This is what the Church means when she teaches that we are made in the image and likeness of God. We learn to see Jesus as the Bridegroom, who shows himself upon the Cross as the beloved spouse of the Church. We find that the love of men and women in marriage becomes a sign of the love of Christ and the Church. And we listen with hope as we begin to see traces of the wedding feast of the Lamb, the final union of God and humanity, in marriage itself. Meditating on the story of salvation, a young person deathly afraid of communication can discover a God who desperately wants to commune with men and women—a God who wants us to fall in love.

In chapter 4, I offer a close reading of the marriage rite itself. In the exchange of vows, man and woman consecrate their love to God. This is a remarkable claim of the Church! Through speaking aloud their promises before God, each other, and the Church, the couple allows their love to become an instrument of God's love. Their love for one another is a manifestation of Jesus' own love dwelling in the world. The wedding rings function for the couple as a sign of this permanent, sacramental bond. The Church now sees in the couple the very love that the Church herself is called toward. At the same time, the couple is called to become what they have received in the sacrament: the love of Christ poured out for the sanctification of the world. The Holy Spirit guides the couple toward an even deeper communion with God, one another, and the world.

In chapter 5, I turn our attention to the Nuptial Blessing. This blessing of husband and wife locates the union of husband and wife in the Eucharist. This means that the couple lives out their married life most fully through their eucharistic life. Through regular participation in the Mass, the couple receives and learns to imitate Christ's sacrificial love in their marriage. This formation into self-gift is manifested in the couple's openness to life and to fruitfulness in every dimension of their marriage and family. The communion of love that the couple experienced on their wedding day spills over into the most mundane of practices: caring for children, paying bills, feeding the hungry, and laughing with one another. This sanctification of the commonplace is at the heart of marriage, as every dimension of human love becomes a sweet offering to God.

Chapter 6, written as a letter addressed to the young adult readers of this book, serves as a conclusion. It shows once more how the communion of love at the heart of marriage can serve as an antidote to the discord of the hookup culture. Certainly many of my students have been suspicious of the Church's opposition to hookup culture. As long as there is mutual consent in the sexual act, they see hooking up as an okay practice. The goal of this last chapter is not to convince such students that they're wrong. Instead, the goal is to present the truth, goodness, and beauty of marriage in such a way that they are invited to see that in the Catholic imagination, hooking up is not enough. We are made for a more intimate communion with God and with one another. This conclusion could serve as a general introduction to the book for those suspicious of its thesis.

A separate appendix at the end features implications of this work for marriage formation. Rather than provide a comprehensive plan for those involved in this work, I give six principles for using the marriage liturgy as a source for healing the hookup culture. I do not propose a universal program for marriage formation, one that will work in every parish and diocese. I simply seek to guide those leading these programs in thinking through a process of formation grounded in a spirituality of communion that begins in early adolescence and ends at death.

A Word about Audience

This book is intended for four audiences. First, it is written for young adults interested in examining an alternative culture to hooking up. Rather than partake in the hookup culture, you can create new stories grounded in God's saving action in the world. You can engage in practices that make creation a place where divine love can dwell. Even those of you who are not proximately preparing for marriage need your imaginations reformed to hope for something more—for what love and marriage in communion with the triune God can be.

Second, this book is written for young couples either preparing for marriage or recently married. Many of you have participated in the hookup culture. Perhaps you're unaware of how that culture has shaped your imagination, something you may only discover three, five, or ten years into your marriage. Perhaps one partner is addicted to pornography, using it to escape from the authentic communication that must take place in the nuptial union. This book seeks to provide an early intervention, before crisis hits. The liturgy you're about to celebrate or recently celebrated can still become for you a rich well of story and practice that forms the basis of a happy marriage. It can be the counter liturgy that leads to nuptial fruitfulness.

Third, it is written for couples in more mature marriages who have their own children to worry about. Long-married couples, while perhaps not reared in the hookup culture, do live in it now. Middle-aged men and women can grow tired of their spouses, seeking out affairs with others to experience a thrilling moment that reminds them of the heady days of falling in love. They can enter into nonsexual extramarital relationships involving emotional adultery, where they share their lives more with a coworker than with their spouse. They may look at pornography, as a way of experiencing sexual excitement, entering a fantasy world different from the mundane love life shared with their spouse. The marriage liturgy can function as a medicine in each of these cases, calling married couples back to the nuptial mystery that is part of their lives. For those couples who remain deeply in love, the hope is that this book enriches your own nuptial love, your sense of the daily gift of mature married love. And as you immerse yourself in this book, you'll discover strategies for enriching the imagination of your own children.

Lastly, this book is written for those responsible for marriage formation at the parish and diocesan level. My own marriage formation was almost bereft of spiritual formation. We were cautioned by the lay minister who was forming us about the risks of getting married too young. Our interest in creating a home suffused with spiritual values was treated as religious extremism. On our marriage preparation retreat, we were taught to communicate with one another, instructed to develop a budget, and given a strong pitch for Natural Family Planning. But we were never asked to contemplate the meaning of the marriage bond we were about to enter into. We were told that we would be ministers of the sacrament, but nothing was mentioned about what our act of consecration meant—that our love was now transfigured through the sacrifice of Christ. Marriage formation that does not bypass spiritual formation is essential if marriage and family life are to become a catalyst for the New Evangelization.

At the end of each chapter, there is a series of questions and suggested activities intended to help individuals or couples appropriate the insights of this book. Liturgical prayer is about the transformation of our memories, our understanding, and our will. Without exercises for our imagination and will, we may feel sated by contemplating the beauty of marriage but forget to reform our actions to live out the Gospel. In each chapter, the last question or exercise, marked "For Marriage Formation," is directed to those involved in marriage formation.

This book is dedicated to my beloved spouse, Kara O'Malley. The surprise for me of mature married love is that I discover through a nearly unimaginable grace that I love you, my spouse, more each day. For the gift of your friendship, your beauty, your motherhood, for your very existence that taught me how to love, I give thanks. Every insight in this book comes from living out the story of divine love with you. And any fallacy is caused by my own hardness of heart, which has been softened through your self-giving love. As we heard sung at our wedding years ago,

> May the LORD bless you from Zion;
> may you see Jerusalem's prosperity
> all the days of your life,
> and live to see your children's children.
> (Ps 128:5–6a)

I hope to receive this blessing more every day. And the blessing of getting to sleep in together now and again.

1.

Hookup Culture

It's eleven o'clock Friday night on a college campus. Students are participating in various forms of recreation after a week full of classes and extracurricular activities. Some are chatting on the quad, taking advantage of the rare warmth of the late-autumn Midwest night. Others are returning from a basketball game. Many of the men are "pregaming" as they get ready to go out for the night. They are playing video games while drinking large quantities of cheap beer that they purchased with fake IDs and then hauled in from the student parking lot in a gym bag. Eventually, they'll change into their party uniform of khaki shorts or pants and a collared shirt. But there are games to play first. And drinking. Always drinking.

The women are also pregaming while getting ready together, taking shots they smuggled onto campus. Of course, hard alcohol has been banned from campus. But if your door is shut, if you're quiet enough, who will know? They're wearing whatever is the fashionable "going-out" outfit. It's a warm night so they won't need to worry about being too cold as they walk around campus looking for parties.

After eleven thirty, the parties are really starting. Most of the festivities are happening in the male dorm rooms on campus. In very small rooms, the lights are turned off, the music is turned up, and sixty undergraduates gather in a space that is normally too small even for the two people who live there. In a corner are a relatively meager supply of cheap beer and a punch consisting mostly of cheap hard liquor. Few students will need more than this, having achieved optimal drunkenness while pregaming. Those students lucky enough to find an option other than the humid hellscape of dorm parties head to off-campus parties, where there is more space, more alcohol, and less risk of getting in trouble with college authorities.

As the night goes on, these young men and women reach peak drunkenness. Some are making out on the dance floor in a dark corner. Some have left the parties after texting their "friend with benefits" for an evening booty call. Two students have found another room to hook up in and the other party-goers can't believe it's *finally* happening. Many just leave, tired of the drinking, exhausted by the music, and head to a twenty-four-hour eatery to sober up before going to bed. Those who have gone off campus don't have to worry about university rules governing when members of the opposite sex can visit dorm rooms. Their parties extend even later into the night when it is easier to find private rooms for hooking up.

There will be collateral damage. Some men and women who hook up this night will quickly regret the decision in the light of day; they will have cheated on boyfriends and girlfriends either on campus or at home. Some will have had sex for the first time this evening in a drunken stupor, barely able to remember what happened. In the haziness of the night, there will have been sexual assaults—many of which will go unreported. A victim will step forward and be forced to relive the awful night during various disciplinary hearings. And an email about the assault will go out to the college community in the coming weeks, resounding once more the refrain that sexual assault is an offense often perpetrated by friends and acquaintances.

The next morning (what the rest of us would call early afternoon), the dining halls are full of tales. Tables of men regale each other with details of their evening's conquests. Some brag about their skills as wingmen, about getting three or four of their friends laid. Such claims need not be true as long as they're proclaimed with vigor. Groups of women are also talking about their evening out. But the tone is different because women who spend the night in men's rooms are subject to the "walk of shame"—wearing their party clothes from the evening before in broad daylight on their way home. There is no equivalent of the walk of shame for men, since their hookup is a matter of pride. Women who hook up with many men get reputations for being easy. Men who hook up with lots of women are objects of envy for the citizens of bro-town.

Tonight, there will be more parties. Many of the previous evening's hookups will happen once again as fresh alcohol flows and the music begins to bump. Men and women will become new friends with benefits—a status that will be implicit until one of them has the courage to start a DTR ("defining the relationship") talk. All the while, students will be complaining to one another: Why is there no dating on campus? Why can't I find a guy or girl who wants to commit? Why isn't there romance? When these men and women leave college, moving to Chicago, New York, Portland, or Des Moines, they'll discover that the same endemic behaviors exist in each of these cities. Sure, the dating pool will be larger. But the cities are infected by the same hookup culture that so many of these students seek to leave behind when they graduate.

The Sexual Market

The stark account above compiles various stories I've heard from undergraduates over the years at Boston College, Notre Dame, and Newman Centers or college campus ministries throughout the country. Obviously, this apocalyptic scene of alcohol-fueled partying is not the normative experience of every student. Many Catholic students avoid this scene altogether, finding alternative ways to spend Friday and Saturday nights. Some of my nonreligious students quickly find a boyfriend or a girlfriend, delighting in normal dating practices like making dinner together and then watching a movie. Some navigate the hookup culture without too many wounds, making out on a dance floor just once before learning from the regret. The idea that colleges are places where everyone is hooking up all the time is an exaggeration perpetuated by marketers who know that sex sells.

The problem with hookup culture isn't so much that everyone is participating in it. It's that it becomes the cultural liturgy by which young adults learn to think about both dating and mating. Recall what I said about a cultural liturgy in the introduction to this book. A cultural liturgy is a series of socially acceptable practices that form us into a way of life. It tells us a story about what we're supposed to do with our bodies. In order to understand what a hookup is, it's necessary for us to examine the practice of the hookup, where it comes from, and what kind of stories the hookup culture tells about dating, love, and ultimately marriage.

Donna Freitas characterizes a hookup as consisting of three dimensions: it includes some form of sexual intimacy, it is brief, and it is purely physical and thus lacking significant communication.[1] The absence of communication in the hookup is particularly troubling. As Freitas writes:

The brevity of a hookup also serves to show how casual a person is about his or her partner. Many students believe they are supposed to regard the hookup as casual—short, and useful, like an afternoon snack for warding off hunger or a workout for staying in shape. Extreme brevity gets sex off one's "To Do" list, and for men, means faster gains in the numbers. Sleepovers and walks of shame are still practiced a fair amount, but the goal remains to avoid any morning interaction. A student leaves before the person wakes up, ideally, so the social contract of not caring about one's partner can be more easily maintained.[2]

The hookup is characterized by a live-and-let-live attitude toward romance, dating, and sexuality in general. In private settings, students may bemoan the lack of seriousness in romance. But in public, they're careful to avoid looking like they care too much. Sexuality and romance are to be treated lightly, as if both are not that big of a deal.

Sociologist Mark Regnerus has argued persuasively that over the last several decades there has been a transformation of both the dating market and the marriage market due to the cheapening of sex. For Regnerus, we can look at sexual activity as an economy of sorts. For the most part, he writes, men value sex more highly than women. This claim does not mean that women shun sex. It simply means that men are more likely to engage in sex if it is offered, even if such sex occurs outside a committed relationship. Summarizing a study in their work *Premarital Sex in America: How Young Americans Meet, Mate, and Think about Marriage*, Regnerus and Jeremy Uecker write:

> Researchers oversaw a unique experiment in which attractive young male and female researchers separately approached other-sex strangers on a college campus, expressed their attraction to them, and then made one of three randomly selected requests: would you go out with me tonight, would

you come over to my apartment tonight, or would you go to bed with me tonight? Fully 75 percent of men—but not a single woman—agreed to the last of these, the invitation to casual sex.[3]

Among those currently in a heterosexual relationship, 52 percent of men claim that they would like more sex in their relationship, while only 29 percent of women make the same claim.[4] When ashleymadison.com (the website that connects married men and women to have affairs) was hacked, journalists discovered that 1,492 women had opened their mailboxes to read a received message compared to 20 million men.[5]

Historically, Regnerus argues, women have been the sexual gatekeepers for men. This argument makes sense. For women, the cost of sex has traditionally been quite high: the possibility of pregnancy. Among men, sex meant a moment of sexual delight with few repercussions if one used protection to avoid sexually transmitted diseases. For women, cheap sex might well have meant the responsibility of raising a child. For this reason, most women and their families ensured that significant commitment was secured from the man—namely, marriage and the responsibilities of fatherhood—before women would engage in sex. Dating itself was considered an innovation in the 1920s, one where women rather than their families were tasked with enforcing male commitment. As author Caitlin Flanagan comments, "it was the girls' responsibility to set and enforce the standards of how much sexual activity should take place on each date."[6] Much of the courtship ritual was intended for the woman to test the commitment of the man, assessing whether he could be a responsible father—someone capable of holding down a job, someone worth spending the rest of her life with.

This account of dating may sound old-fashioned, but it was precisely the "old-fashioned" nature of dating that made sex costly. For example, my father-in-law's first date with my mother-in-law was an icon of this old-fashioned courtship. Early in the morning on the day of the Notre Dame–USC football game in 1969, he trekked from his dorm, Lyon's Hall, on the Notre Dame campus to Saint Mary's College—a twenty-five minute walk—to pick up the woman who would be his wife for their first date. They went to a party in Lyon's Hall and then headed out to watch the Irish tie Southern Cal 14–14. Following the game, they went to dinner, after which my father-in-law walked my mother-in-law back to her dorm. He then walked back that evening to walk her back and forth to Notre Dame for a concert. Consider how much walking—and thus talking—was required for my father-in-law to express his interest in my mother-in-law (he definitely got his steps in that day!). Think about how public this act of dating was. The courtship rituals surrounding dating, although perhaps archaic, elevated the cost of both romance and sex. A guy couldn't just text a woman in the middle of the night, ask her to come over, and wait to see what happened.

What led to cheaper sex? The introduction of widely available hormonal contraception changed the dating market, making it far easier for men and women alike to have sex whenever they wanted. Regnerus writes:

> Since pregnancy can be easily prevented now—a reality we take for granted today, but one that was unimaginable not so long ago—having sex and thinking about or committing to marry are two very different things today. Now we have a split mating market, one corner of which is for people primarily looking and hoping for sex with no strings attached (NSA) and the other corner of which is for people interested in making the strongest of commitments (marriage), with a rather large territory in between comprised of significant relationships of varying commitment and duration. Marriage is still widely considered to be expensive, by which I mean that it is . . . not entered into lightly, and is costly in terms of fidelity,

time, finances, and personal investment. Sex, meanwhile, has become comparatively cheap. Not that hard to get.[7]

The hookup culture has further lowered the cost of sex. The first sexual encounter between couples who do not hook up during their first meeting tends to occur within the first two to six weeks. In 2001–2002, the results of a longitudinal study related to the sexual health of young adults concluded. In these survey results, it was determine that among unmarried eighteen- to twenty-three-year-old men, 38.5 percent had had five or more sexual partners; 36.6 percent of women claimed the same number.[8] Not surprisingly, this same survey determined that fewer than 6 percent of men and women would approach the altar as virgins.[9] We might well surmise that the first numbers noted here have continued to increase.

Even those who do not participate in the hookup culture are still affected by the cheapening of sex in the dating market. They grow up watching television and films in which it is normative for young, attractive men and women to engage in sex soon after meeting. They hear about friends who have participated in drunken hookups and who have parlayed such hookups into long-term relationships. And when they go out on a date, it is likely that the person on the other side of the table expects easy access to sex early in the relationship. A friend of mine recently heard on a date: "We don't have to have sex on the third date."

The decline of the old courtship rituals means that even if you're not interested in hooking up, you're still trying to date men and women who do not know how to communicate interest. Hooking up in the end isn't really just about sensual desire. Rather, it is destructive because it leads to the weakening of communication and to the decline of intimacy whereby we learn to know and to love the other person face-to-face.

Tinder, Cheap Sex, and the End of Communication

The hookup is thus a symptom of a larger problem—the exchange of authentic communion for immediate sexual intimacy. The cheapening of sex has been facilitated by the rising popularity of online dating and apps like Tinder. In a 2015 *Vanity Fair* article, Nancy Jo Sales describes a Manhattan bar in the rough-and-tumble age of electronically facilitated cheap sex:

> It's a balmy night in Manhattan's financial district, and at a sports bar called Stout, everyone is Tindering. The tables are filled with young women and men who've been chasing money and deals on Wall Street all day, and now they're out looking for hookups. Everyone is drinking, peering into their screens and swiping on the faces of strangers they may have sex with later that evening.[10]

Tinder deforms romance into a quick glance at another person's body on a screen. If the user of the app finds the person attractive, they swipe right. If they find them unattractive, left. When two people both swipe right on each other, it's a match. There will be few romantic comedies about the short-term relationships that are initiated on Tinder.

Tinder is the ideal technological tool for facilitating hookups. There is no romance before meeting up, no exchange of messages containing at least the pretense of flirtation. The swipe right sends out a wordless digital signal meaning "You're hot." Sometimes, as Sales describes in her article, there is a message sent: "Wanna F*&$?"

By now many, if not most, of us have either heard of or experienced success in the world of online dating. Nonetheless, we should examine more closely the kinds of habits that are formed through such online forums. When I was dating in college, there was a limited number of human beings I could actually meet. I was restricted to very specific geographic places like Notre Dame, Indiana, or Knoxville, Tennessee. Online dating and apps like Tinder end that limitation. Now, there is a seemingly infinite number of possible partners only a swipe or click away. In some sense, this is a good. It means that people can meet one another who otherwise wouldn't—like a colleague's son and his wife who met on Catholic Match. But the near-endless supply of potential mates entices men and women struggling in their relationships to wonder if the grass is greener elsewhere. When a relationship ends, there is always someone else to click or swipe on.

But of course, those swiping or clicking may not be pursuing a long-term relationship at all. They may be hoping for no-strings-attached sex. As Regnerus comments on sexual economics in the age of Tinder: "The most relevant thing about online dating is not its ability to match preferences before you meet but rather that it enables people to sort through sexual and romantic 'options' more efficiently."[11] Online dating and Tinder make it easier to objectify a partner, turning them into an avatar linked to our own desires. For many, this desire will be fulfilled in a cheap sexual encounter, a hookup with no strings attached. The men that Sales highlights in her article in *Vanity Fair* appreciate that apps like Tinder enable them to proposition not one or two women per night but fifteen or twenty. Notice that it's not the particular person who matters in the sexual encounter. It's simply her availability as a sexual partner.

The tendency toward no-strings-attached sex is not the only problem with online dating. Remember that the hookup is marked fundamentally by the refusal to communicate; it requires ambiguity as well as a refusal to recognize the other person as anything more than a source of physical pleasure. Before the advent of dating apps, the text message served as an efficient invitation for the hookup because it could say just enough without saying too much. The late-night booty call, no longer requiring voice-to-voice contact, could be initiated through as few as three words: "Hey! You awake?"

But the text message required at least some knowledge of the other person. It presumed enough of a relationship that one had the other person's phone number on hand. At some point in time, the interested party had to get to know the other person well enough to ask, "Could I have your number?" Among those Tindering, this last trace of intimacy is eliminated. All that remains is the expression of desire for the other, a furtive glance across a bar now accomplished through packets of data communicated through cell tower or wireless network to receiver. There is no face-to-face contact—only the thrill of being the object of an unknown person's desire. Whether or not the liaison works out, there are more swipes to be accomplished in the future.

We have to admit the possibility that this severing of authentic communication in dating will have long-term effects on some young adults who do not gaze upon the face of a potential beloved but instead see only an avatar, an image constructed by the Tinder user. My female friends who have used Catholic Match have suffered from a different, though similarly objectifying, approach to dating, one in which men are not looking for an encounter with a woman but seeking to examine her doctrinal orthodoxy before they've asked where she grew up. Love doesn't typically begin through either an anonymous sexual encounter or the Inquisition.

In neither case do we romance the other person. We don't meet them first for coffee, discovering a beauty that is communicated through their living presence. Dating becomes marketing a brand rather than communicating with another human being. And this confusion wreaks havoc on human relationships. After all, no matter how much we love our MacBook, we don't need to consider its nonexistent feelings when we purchase it or decide that we would prefer a PC. But when we're dating in this market-driven manner, the person whose image we swiped right on is a living, breathing human being with a memory, an imagination, hopes, dreams, desires, and affections. Apps like Tinder and many online dating sites create spaces where the dating market becomes a literal market for human beings looking to "consume" rather than seek communion with each other.

The Cost of Pornographic Sex

If it is a requirement of the hookup to eliminate any significant act of communication beyond the physical encounter, then pornography is the most efficient form of hooking up. We no longer even need another human being, but can gaze upon naked flesh in the privacy of our homes. All we need is access to the Internet.

The use of pornography is very high. Extraordinarily high. The Austin Institute for the Study of Family and Culture released a survey in 2014 that studied the prevalence of pornography use in the United States.[12] Among eighteen- to thirty-nine-year olds, 46 percent of surveyed men used pornography in the last week. Sixteen percent of women also said they did. Twenty-four percent of men said they had viewed pornography in the last day.[13] What does this mean? Notre Dame has 8,448 undergraduates on campus, roughly 51 percent of them male. Thus, it is likely that over a thousand of the undergraduate men on Notre Dame's campus have looked at porn today.

The porn that these undergraduates are viewing is not your grandfather's or even your father's porn. I worked at a book and video store in East Tennessee while in high school in the late nineties. In our video section, we rented pornos in opaque packaging. We also had a small section of pornography magazines covered in green plastic that even the most devoted and desirous of adolescent men couldn't see through. Once a month or so, I would rent out one of these videos to someone. The social cost of renting a porn video at my store was high. Everyone in the store could see you wander through the adult video section, attempting to discern what film you would devote the coming hours to watching. Everyone also knew what you would be doing as you watched this film. You then had to deal with the clerk, who had to make sure that you knew what you were renting, saying the absurd title aloud just in case anyone in the store had missed seeing you enter the adult video section. You then left the store marked as a high-functioning pervert by the store's employees and patrons.

Today, my male undergraduate students never run the gauntlet of a single video store. From the time they're in middle school, pornography websites seek them out using an algorithm to estimate their age while they surf the web (think about the last time you Googled a jacket you wanted to buy, only to discover that Facebook and other online ads were now advertising this jacket to you)—if you're going to get a young person addicted to porn, it's best to start early. Some of these sites are a more revealing version of the *Sports Illustrated Swimsuit Edition,* dispensing with the final traces of clothing that the magazine calls a bikini. Other sites are more violent, featuring images of men ejaculating into the faces of women. Anal penetration in these videos is presumed. As a person descends into the dark recesses of these sites, the user will discover still more violent pornography called "gonzo" porn. The user will encounter pornography featuring women who are dressed as young girls. The woman is always sexually available to a man who engages in sex with little emotion.

The sexual education of many men today, and their formation into romance, will unfold through watching, often addictively, this violent pornography. In her 2006 work *Pornified: How Pornography Is Transforming Our Lives, Our Relationships, and Our Families*, journalist Pamela Paul writes:

> Pornography is frequently the first place boys learn about sex and gain an understanding of their own sexuality, whims, preferences, and predilections—their desires unfiltered and informed by whatever the pornography they watch has to offer. As adolescents, many boys learn through pornography to direct their sexual feelings toward the opposite sex, to explain the source of their desires and the means to satisfy them. . . . Whether mediated by outside sources or not, the pornography lesson is nothing if not straightforward. . . . Pornography depicts sex as an easy process that provides a welcome refuge from the tangle of sexual politics teenagers encounter in the real world.[14]

Pornography functions as a cultural liturgy for the men who watch it. They learn that women are always open to their sexual advances. They learn that sex is necessarily violent, and that women delight in abusive practices such as anal sex and the forced swallowing of semen. The former, not just devoid of pleasure for women but actually painful, has become a relatively common sexual practice in recent years partially through the influence of pornography and men's magazines that explore exotic sexual acts and positions.

Women are not exempt from the effects of pornography of course. First, an increasing number of women are now viewing pornography themselves. As noted above, 16 percent of women have looked at pornography in the last week. Second, the majority of women who do not look at pornography still end up dating men who do—men who try to influence these women to watch pornography with them as foreplay for sex. Women may fall for men addicted to pornography, and this will affect their future relationship. Third, although pornography was once the domain of the pervert, it now influences mainstream culture. Lingerie shops are scattered throughout the mall. Even young girls are encouraged to get a Brazilian wax, eliminating all pubic hair from their bodies in the style of many porn stars. Magazines that cater to women show them precisely how to look sexy and to provide for their man's needs in the bedroom (every cover of *Cosmopolitan* teases at least one story about how to please him sexually). Gail Dines, an academic who studies pornography, describes the porn-derived marketing directed at women from a young age: "The low-slung jeans, the short skirt that rides up our legs as we sit down, the thong, the tattoo on the lower back, the pierced belly button, the low-cut top that shows cleavage, the high heels that contour our calves, and the pouting glossed lips all conspire to make us look like a bargain-basement version of the real thing."[15] Often in the name of liberation, women are reduced to objects for sexual consumption, real-life porn stars that satisfy the male gaze.

No one is shielded from this influence. Before marrying my wife, I had never watched pornography. I had never seen a pornography magazine. But I had watched television. And from my time of watching TV, I came to expect that the bedroom of married couples would be a very sexy place. Entering into marriage, I assumed that my wife would want to wear a unique piece of lingerie each evening. She didn't. I learned from my wife that lingerie is not actually the most comfortable clothing to sleep in; at least not as comfortable as an old T-shirt and a pair of shorts. I learned that my spouse might not be interested in having sex every night but might be more interested in just sleeping. Because of my assumptions, formed through watching television and movies rated no more adult than R, the early days of our marriage were filled with conflict over our expectations of what married sexuality would look like.

The cost of cheap, pornographic sex is quite high. Many men cease desiring a living and breathing woman altogether. They prefer masturbating before hypersexualized and violent images on the Internet. Porn ends up substituting for real relationships. Regnerus and Uecker write:

> The widespread availability and popularity of porn—obviously partnered with masturbation—serves to drive down the price of sex with real women (without their realizing it). It . . . encourages women as well as men to have sex earlier than they otherwise might have. . . . One of the obvious concerns about porn is that it functions for men as a substitute for a real person, and women realize this. It can curb men's ability to relate to women by diminishing their interest—and perhaps more importantly their *patience*—in doing so.[16]

Crudely put, when sex in a hookup culture has been reduced to the purely physical pleasure of the encounter, when communication is devalued, then it's easier to masturbate on one's own than to deal with someone who laughs and cries, who has good days and bad days, who wants to be listened to and perhaps romanced. You know, a real person.

Conclusion

The effect of hookup culture on young couples is consequential. Hookup culture intentionally brackets communication in relationships. It encourages the reduction of one's partner to a sexual object for pleasure. It leads to an understanding of sexuality as a consumer exchange. It culminates in the cheapest sex of all, self-pleasure through masturbation before pornographic images. It is this culture that wounds the young couples who come to the local parish for marriage formation. It is this anti-liturgy that many of them have celebrated in their daily practices of pornography addiction, of the pursuit of sexual partners, of avoiding communication at all costs. Many of these young people had sex well before talking about dating because they saw the conversation as too intimate.

But the ones who darken the church door seeking to marry are the unusual ones. One demographer estimates that only one out of three people in their early twenties will ever get married.[17] Why would they? They have had access to sex from a young age. Many women have problems finding men who are interested in marriage since the availability of cheap sex has led to an extended and sometimes permanent adolescence.[18]

These young people have also embraced the narrative that in order to be married, one must achieve perfect compatibility with a spouse. As Regnerus writes:

> Commitment is just not needed to access sex today in the split, gender-imbalanced modern mating pool. Women no longer need men to socially, culturally, and economically succeed in life. In step, there is less motivation for men to "be noble" and respect women's interests. Cheap sex slows down the road to marriage, makes its would-be participants think twice about it, and draws their attention toward consumption rather than production.[19]

If the trend continues, it's possible that those who marry—Christian or not—will function as minority members of society, remnants of a strange, faded culture that valued monogamy and family life.

The Church must respond to what seems like an impossible situation. Some might want to set up a nice little bunker, raising our children apart from the rest of society, hopeful that we will be the foundation of a new world order. But that's not Catholicism. Instead, we must face the cultural liturgy of the hookup directly, offering a reasonable account of love. We have the medicine the world wants and needs.

For the sake of future Christian marriage, Catholic colleges and universities in particular need to find a way of countering hookup culture. But too often, these institutions are primarily concerned with avoiding litigation by enforcing consent laws. They teach students to pursue consent in each sexual encounter and train men and women to protect against sexual assault at on- and off-campus parties. Such conversations are important insofar as they make students conscious that their assumptions about sexuality are inadequate.

But discussions of consent are not enough. Such narratives don't offer the coherent account of love and marriage that students crave. They don't deal with the fear of intimacy and communion that paralyzes so many young men and women. They don't address how the abuse of alcohol at many dorm parties covers over the fear of authentic encounter with another. The antidote to hooking up isn't solely a more careful use of our sexuality. Instead, the real remedy is discovering what it means to love in the first place.

Catholic colleges, universities, and campus ministries can and should do better. Catholicism offers a rich and reasonable account of love and marriage that can serve as a treatment for those addicted to the hookup. For in Catholicism, love is always about communion.

Exercises

1. Hookup culture is not just about sex; it writes a story about love on our bodies through our behaviors. How have the practices of hookup culture formed your own understanding of love and sexuality?
2. Hooking up depends on a lack of communication. Whether you've been married for twenty years, are engaged, or are just dating someone, think about your own practices of

communication. In which areas of your relationship do you communicate well? In which do you communicate poorly? What will you do to change this? In avoiding communication, hookup culture mostly avoids dating. If you're single, go on a date. If you're married, engaged, or dating, set up two singles you know on a date. Don't just send them alone—make it a couples' date.

The date doesn't have to be expensive or involve a fancy dinner. Instead, it should be oriented toward creating an opportunity for conversation. Try to make the date last for at least an hour and a half. Make sure you choose a public place for the date (not a dorm room). Ask good questions throughout the date (it's okay to prepare some of these questions beforehand). The key purpose of dating, especially early on, is finding a way to communicate with another person!

3. **For Marriage Formation:** Begin to reimagine an approach to marriage formation that would heal those formed in the hookup culture (perhaps it's you!). What would this approach include?

2.

Love as Communion

Kara, my then girlfriend, was preparing to take a trip to Ireland for fall break. Before she left, I planned to tell her "I love you." While I had uttered these words countless times to my parents, my grandparents, and my brother, this was the first time I would say them to her. We had been dating for two and a half months. I had already visited her family during the first two weeks of our relationship. During the week or so we had been apart, we had spent hours each evening on the phone with one another, sharing every thought. We had had one significant spat where she considered breaking up with me. And now, as she prepared to board a plane for Dublin, it was time to say those words.

We walked down to the Grotto at the University of Notre Dame and kneeled before the candles lit in honor of Mary just as we had on our first date. We each lit a candle, praying for one another. And then we sat on a bench to talk for a bit before we said goodbye for ten infinitely long days. I was tense, afraid that my offering of love would not be returned. Perhaps, I would hear "I like you, too" in response. Or worse, "Thank you."

In the middle of normal conversation, like a balloon expelling air, I exclaimed, "I love you." Kara looked at me and replied, "I love you, too." I breathed a sigh of relief and prepared to offer her a short discourse on what this mutual profession of love meant to me (the perils of dating a philosopher-theologian). If our friend Kevin had not suddenly appeared to interrupt this moment of romance, my wife-to-be would have been subjected to a mini-lecture on Dante, French existentialism, and St. Augustine.

I returned to my dorm, somehow changed by this briefest of exchanges with my wife-to-be. Before that evening, I had been aware of the love of my parents, who gave me life, who cared for me as I grew older, who prayed for me each and every evening. I knew that my friends loved me, willing my good at every moment of the day, sharing with me the deepest values. But now, I knew that there was a woman in the world who, though she didn't have to, freely loved me with her total being. And I understood that there was a person whom I loved with my whole being. It felt as though the air itself had been infused with pure possibility, with hope, with gift. *She loved me. And I loved her.*

The Problem of Defining Love

As we discovered in chapter 1, the hookup culture depends on fear of or simply disinterest in communication, and thus communion, with a living, breathing human being. Hooking up divorces the act of sex from the experience of love. That human beings desire love is undeniable. We want to be loved by our parents, by our friends, and eventually by our spouse. We want spousal love to be total, to involve every part of our lives. Yet we need to ask ourselves the most basic of questions: what do we mean when we say that we love someone?

Before we answer this question, it's important to clarify terminology around love that is used throughout this book. At times, I write about natural, true, or romantic love. Here, I mean the kind of love accessible to anyone whether they're Christian or not. Those with a religious background are not the only ones who experience this love. And the Sacrament of Marriage in the Church presumes the presence of this love in every marriage. At other times, I will use more specific terms like spousal, conjugal, or sacramental love. These terms are used to speak about the kind of love that those who enter into the Sacrament of Marriage experience. Conjugal love, as one might suppose, is not related to sex (we often think about a "conjugal" visit in prison). Rather, "conjugal" love is a love that has "bound" husband and wife together.

Still, even if we're careful with our terminology, it is no easy task to define the experience of love. Some will describe love as a feeling, a passionate attraction to another person. Others see romantic love as the purest form of willing the good of another. We know that we can be wrong about love, discovering over the course of a relationship that we did not love the other person as much as we loved the experience of being in love. We can mistake sexual attraction for love and find out that once the initial desire that led us into the arms of this man or this woman fades, nothing remains.

Nonetheless, if we bypass the task of defining love, there is no ground for understanding marriage. We're left groping in the dark, dependent on the wavering of feelings that move hither and thither. Often, this is how we understand love early in our lives. Adolescents and young adults "fall in love" at the drop of a hat. If I could peek in on my twenty-year-old self, I would encounter a young man listening to the angsty love songs of the Irish singer Damien Rice, trying to imagine how he could live without the return gift of love of the young woman he has most recently fallen for. I could leave my twenty-year-old self for six weeks and return to the same scene, but with a different woman now as the source of the angst. At this stage, I understood love principally as a personal experience. I knew that I was "in love" when I "felt" in love.

But love is not merely a construct of our personal feelings. We know this. Falling in love feels like an objective fact to us. We fall in love with a real person. The terror that accompanies our first confession of love to our beloved is there for a reason. To tell our beloved that we love them means something more than that we "feel" nice around them. It means that we want to share our whole self with that person. And we'd really like that person to share their whole self in return. The possibility of being rejected, of offering ourselves and not receiving love in return, is demonstrably terrifying.

Love involves our feelings, our desires, and our interior life (what philosophers might call *subjectivity*). But it is not *limited* to such subjectivity, because when I fall in love, I love a real, concrete person. When I was engaged, I knew my fiancée loved me not because of some general feeling I had about her, but because I experienced the depths of her love when she came over after a long day of work to nurse me back to health from a stomach bug that had wreaked havoc on me. I was a shell of myself, pale as a ghost, lying in a fetal position on the couch. She came over and initiated a discipline of rehydration by giving me a single ice cube every ten minutes. She stayed with me until I was ready for bed although to do so was to risk sickness herself. We recognize love because it manifests itself to us not merely as a feeling of passion but as an event—as a series of moments in which our beloved reveals to us the truth that means everything to us: someone loves me!

Love as Drama

Love may be a problem for us insofar as we cannot immediately understand it. But because it is an objective fact, we can study it. St. John Paul II's writings on marriage, sexuality, and love are a helpful resource in clarifying our thinking about the nature of love. When he was still a philosopher known as Karol Wojtyla teaching in Lublin, Poland, he wrote in his work *Love and Responsibility* that "love is . . . a drama in the sense that it is always a happening and at the same time an acting."[1]

Think for a moment about the theater. When we attend a play or a musical, a story unfolds in front of us. Actors in the play take upon themselves roles that they do not construct, lines that are given to them to perform. The play happens, revealing to us truths about the goodness of life, about the fragility of relationships, and about love. We find ourselves taken up into a plot, into another world, that feels as real as can be. Each time actors perform a play, the event happens anew in our midst.

But the theater is not merely about contemplating truths from afar, for those who attend the play are invited to let the affections of the actors become their own, while the actors take on the personas written into the drama. During my junior year in college, while studying abroad, I was cast as Othello in some scenes we were doing from Shakespeare's play on the stage of the reconstructed Globe Theater. As a novice actor, I initially had a difficult time entering into Othello's character. I memorized my lines and recited them with vigor, with passion, with what I thought was drama. But the director kept correcting me. He made me realize that to play Othello, I had to bring my imagination and will alike into the performance. I had to understand the intense jealousy and despair that led Othello to his tragic murdering of Desdemona. I had to cease being Tim reciting lines from Shakespeare's play and become Othello, letting his will (happily only for the time I was on the stage) become my own.

Love is a drama where there is something that happens that isn't just subjective (it's an encounter with another person). It's an encounter that we have to participate in with our whole hearts including our will. It's an encounter in which we freely give our wills over to another. It is an event in which we discover that there is another person in the world who loves us, and we freely take up this role as beloved, offering our own love as a return gift. Like a play, love involves affections, a rich contemplation of certain values as incarnate in a particular person. Yet it also requires the free gift of our will in return.

When I say that I love my wife, Kara, I really mean two things. First, I mean that I love the person of Kara. In seeing her, I see the goodness of her intelligence, the beauty of a wife and mother who is capable of sacrificial love. I experience her as a supreme gift. Second, in confessing my love for my wife, I also mean that I want to give the entirety of myself to her. It is not enough for me just to look at her beauty, admiring it from afar. I want to enter into the drama of loving my wife, to share a whole life with her.

Love's ability to change our lives, to serve as an event that reorders everything, is the reason that romantic love is so often the subject of music, poetry, literature, and art. Too often, we dismiss this love as trite. Such romantic love, we suspect, is too subjective, too dependent on our feelings. But music, poetry, and art capture for us the totalizing dimension of love. If I look back at my study abroad journal, I will see love poem after love poem written for the many women I thought I loved while studying in England. Part of me wants to roll my eyes at myself (a very hard thing to do). But another part of me sees that such expressions of romantic love, no matter how naïve, were moving me in the right direction. Even romantic love is an experience that involves our whole selves.

In hookup culture, as we saw in chapter 1, this key aspect of interpersonal communion is missing. The more seriously we take love, the more we realize how it enriches every dimension of our lives. When I first fell in love with Kara, I nauseatingly (at least to my friends) talked about her all the time. This totalizing dimension of the drama of love is precisely what inspired medieval poets to portray their relationship with God as one of *eros*, of desire: "Love yearns for the beloved with pure desire; / Love is like perishable fire. / Love purges sin; love brings us home to bliss; / Love sings of joy; love wins the kingly kiss."[2] And it has real consequences for how we view our relationship with God.

The Personalistic Norm

Love, of course, is a very powerful experience. How do we make sure that the experience of our feelings does not overpower the objective act of loving a particular person? This question is an important one. Think about the early days of falling in love, the way our beloved occupies so much of our interior life. We think about them throughout the day. We long to be with them.

My love of Kara began as this kind of love. In the first weeks of our relationship, we spent hours on the phone talking to one another (in a time when people still talked on phones with regularity). When we were apart, I longed simply to hear her voice.

Yet there is a dangerous aspect of the totalizing experience of love. We may find ourselves more attached to the experience of being in love than to the particular person. During our first full semester of dating in college, I often demanded too much from Kara. I wanted her to be fully present to me at all times because of how she made me feel. Yet, in letting myself succumb to the experience of love, I often forgot to love Kara as a person who had her own needs, desires, and thoughts. My subjective experience of being in love had overpowered the objective need to love Kara as a person. I suspect that what I "loved" most about Kara early in our relationship was how she made me feel. That's not yet the fullness of love.

There is another danger to focusing all on subjectivity in love. To elevate the subjective as the principle norm for love would mean that there is no permanence to love. Every time my feelings changed, I would have to reimagine what it means to love. If, for example, I found that I was not thinking about Kara as often as I did in the earliest days of our romance, I could conclude that I had "fallen out of love." Serious problems could result if I based my love of my wife upon such a norm. I would love my wife only if I felt or perceived her as worthy of love. When another woman came along, then I might refocus my attention on her as the next object of my affection. Kara is the best (until she isn't). The result of relying on such fickle feelings would be broken hearts and families. We need an objective norm outside of our feelings to order our affections.

The objective dimension of love is what St. John Paul II calls the *personalistic norm*. In loving someone, we should not merely be affirming that this woman or this man is sexually attractive *to me*. We should not mean that we love how this person makes *me* feel. Instead, when we love someone, we love a real-life person. And we reorient our affections, our desires toward giving ourselves away in love to this person: St. John Paul II wrote that "true love, the kind of love of others worthy of a human person, is that in which our sensory energies and desires are subordinated to a basic understanding of the true worth of the object of our love."[3] We come to recognize that this man or this woman, who exists outside of ourselves, is worthy of love.

Thus, when I love my wife, I don't merely love the experience of being attracted to a beautiful woman. I'm not using her for her intellect alone. I love her as the unique person named Kara. And I seek to give myself entirely to her. Remarkably, as I give myself entirely to her, as I love her and not just the feelings that I have about her, I experience a new flowering of affection, a deeper awareness of the beauty of the values that she brings to our relationship.

Often, the single students whom I find myself counseling mistakenly understand love as a subjective passion. They enter into relationships and are disappointed not to immediately discover a passionate connection (at least not as passionate as they expect it to be). They want every act of dating, of love, to be full of rainbows and roses. They want to star in romantic comedies where there is instantaneous love rather than documentaries where human beings discover love over the course of years. But we fall in love and discover it as totalizing *as* we commit ourselves to loving this person. It is the personalistic norm that makes love both possible and passionate.

For this reason, the personal dimension of love does not mean that love must leave behind all feeling, all sexual desire, or all appreciation of our beloved's values. If love were simply the result of an abstract norm, then it would be a sterile thing indeed. To love my wife, I would just have to hunker down and will myself to obey the norm. Love would be like going to the gym, skipping chocolate during Lent, or trying to will oneself out of bed in the morning. But no one who has fallen in love thinks about it in this manner. Instead, as St. John Paul II argues, when we operate according to the personalistic norm, our affections, our desires, and even our sensuality are healed through the act of love.

Through love, we come to see our beloved as a luminous person, elevated above all other creatures. Dietrich von Hildebrand, a philosopher who influenced St. John Paul II, writes:

> Love is that which gives us sight, revealing to us even the
> faults of the other in their full import and causing us to suf-
> fer because of them. But . . . love reveals to us intuitively
> the whole being of the other in a mysteriously lucid unity.
> It not only shows us individual praiseworthy traits but also
> the particular charm of his individuality as a whole, which
> permeates everything and characterizes the essence of his
> being—a charm which can only be completely understood by
> the complementary person and can have its full significance
> in him alone.[4]

Sure, they have their faults. They leave their socks on the floor.
They chew loudly when they eat cereal. They don't listen as
well as they could. But love isn't about making a pro and con
list about one's beloved. Love is a revelation that the other is
one's beautiful beloved. It is a revelation of a truth: I love *you*.
I want to be involved with you, to give myself to you. Yes, my
particular feelings may change, but such changes do not affect
my ultimate commitment to *you*!

When I say "I love you" to Kara, I really mean the following: I love the way your eyes sparkle when you laugh. I love the
patience you have when mothering our two children. I love the
gift you have for teaching the Christian faith, the creativity you
bring to every act of religious formation. I love the beauty of
your voice, the way you offer it up to God at every family wedding and funeral. I love the way you sacrifice your own sleep
when I'm busy at work, taking care of kids who can certainly
bring us to the point of exhaustion. I could go on probably
forever. But my love is not based on these characteristics of my
spouse. It is not based on the feelings that these values elicit. It
is based on her person: "I love my dear Kara." And when I love
her as a person, then I begin to see everything in a new light.
Love's communion changes everything about my world.

The Freedom of Love

Returning to the image of the theater, love isn't merely about the revelation of a truth. Love is also about action. It's about the will. It is true that eating fries every day will be perilous to one's health. It is true that driving while texting is a dangerous affair. But if we don't exert our wills, we may easily find ourselves doing either or both. As St. Augustine reminds us throughout his writings, we often love the good, but we struggle to accomplish it. In love, this means that we may recognize the dignity of our beloved's personhood, but we may struggle to give our will over to our beloved.

I've met couple after couple in my teaching career who really do love one another. Each person sees his or her beloved as a person of the highest dignity, but is afraid to give everything. They fear that if they committed their whole will to the other person, they would lose control. They want to remain in the theater, but as members of the audience; they're not yet capable of pursuing their vocation as actors. They recognize the truth, but they don't know what to do.

There is something terrifying about committing ourselves to a love that extends beyond the present. When I fell in love with my wife-to-be, it was 2003. Since then, many things have happened. I've changed, moving from a radical extrovert to a functional introvert. My wife has also changed, moving from an introvert to, well, an extreme introvert. Such changes may seem small, but they're linked to the various ways that our individual stories have continued since we've entered marriage. Over those years, we've graduated from college, worked in jobs we've loved and hated, developed new friendships, had our hearts broken by the death of loved ones, and learned more about our own gifts and weaknesses. With all this possibility for individual change, we might ask ourselves, how can I permanently commit myself to a person, give my whole will, my whole self, over to someone who will be different in two years' time? In five years? In fifty years?

St. John Paul II notes that the drama of love consists of a free gift of the will that is constant and never-ending. He writes:

> For love is never something ready-made, something merely "given" to a woman and a man, but at once it is always something "entrusted." It is necessary to look at it this way: love in a sense never "is," but only constantly "becomes," depending on the contribution of each person, on their thorough commitment.[5]

When I love another, I freely give my will over to my beloved. But this self-gift of love is never complete. There is always more to give, more to offer, because we seek to give nothing less than our full selves. This constancy of gift is the adventure of love. When we fall in love, we are not done.

We sometimes forget this. We imagine that in order to love another person forever, to make the step toward marriage, we need to be perfect. We need to have lots of money to have a family, to buy a house. We need to have reached the highest level of our career. We need to have cultivated every dimension of our own character through traveling abroad, graduate school, and service programs. We think getting married means first reaching the heights of love and then offering a commitment. But this isn't how true love works. True love is an adventure in which we find richer depths of love in the act of loving. The more we freely love, the more capacity we have to love.

Only in marriage, in the Church or outside of it, is such freedom possible. Outside of marriage, there is always the possibility that our beloved could leave, so the gift of self is partial, since it has no objective norm to depend on. But as Dietrich von Hildebrand makes clear, "Marriage is a reality in the objective order which is constituted only by a solemn act and presupposes a formal act of the will: the two partners give themselves expressly to each other, fully sanctioning this surrender for their entire lifetime."[6] The permanence of marriage makes it possible for us to participate in a lifelong education in giving our wills over to our beloved. We can be sure that our self-giving love will always be returned in some way.

For many of us, the offering of a vow may seem less than freeing. Wouldn't it be better to have an escape hatch in case our love grows sterile? In case our beloved ceases being lovable? I suspect that many young adults avoid marriage because they do see it as an imposition on their freedom. Marriage means this person forever and always. Marriage means a family, bills, and calling home before heading out to a bar—an end to freedom.

But this notion of freedom is inadequate. It reduces freedom to nothing but the ability to do whatever we want. But that's not really freedom. Is it freeing to let a child put a paperclip into an electric socket? Surely, there's more to freedom than willing what we want.

Freedom is always an encounter with the truth, with norms that exist outside of ourselves. Think about baseball for a moment. Baseball has concrete rules and structures that guide the playing of the game. It is freeing in baseball to know that there is some objective norm, some truth outside of the individual player. If you're tagged, you're out. Only through these norms can you freely play the game of baseball.

This same kind of freedom is available through marriage whether sacramental or not. By pledging myself to another human being, I commit myself to this person for as long as we both shall live. There is now a norm outside of my own desires that can guide my decision-making. I am no longer "free" to romantically love any human being. But now authentic freedom is possible because I can enter into communion with another human being throughout my life. I can give myself to another person, knowing that he or she will return this gift of self for as long as we both shall live. I have been freed from individual desire and now liberated for love unto the end.

This understanding of freedom comes with responsibility. Love involves a reciprocal self-gift, so when Kara and I admitted to one another that we were in love, this required a new tenderness on both of our parts. It necessitated that we pay closer attention to the ways we were tempted to reduce each other to objects for our own personal enjoyment. For me, this meant reining in the expectations I had for Kara. I had a tendency to see love as requiring extraordinary sacrifice. I wanted Kara to make decisions about her life based solely on me. During our senior year of college, I forced conversation after conversation about our future, chats in which I attempted to manipulate Kara into acting as I hoped she would. It was Kara's consistent love that healed me of this tendency. She didn't leave me because I was annoying and loving me was difficult, but rather she respected me, and loved my person by being direct and asking me to stop. She renewed her commitment to me, taking responsibility for my formation in the virtue of love through her willingness to engage in honest conversations about how I might cultivate a more authentic sense of love. Freely taking such responsibility for the good of another does not come immediately; thus, the lifelong permanence of married love is an education into such freedom.

Thus, there is an irony to the freedom of a lifelong commitment. In limiting our possibilities through lifelong commitment and taking on responsibility for the happiness of another person, I am able to love well. The freedom that is available in love is communion with another person.

Sex and Chastity

Of course, love between a man and a woman does involve attraction, a certain undeniable sensual desire. I'll always remember the first time I met my wife. I was singing in a choir at the University of Notre Dame during the summer of 2002. Below me, I saw out of the corner of my eye a beautiful woman. After we finished singing, I found a friend of mine who also knew this young woman. The object of my attraction, I learned, was named Kara. We shook hands, and I introduced myself. She quickly turned away—a fact that I reminded her of when we later began to date. The meeting lasted no longer than five minutes. In fact, my wife has no memory of this meeting. But the encounter changed me. Although we would not see each other for another year after this first meeting, this first attraction was what drew me to her again when we found ourselves working together the next summer. It is what pushed me to spend long nights talking with her in the company of friends, hoping that she would return my interest.

I still think my wife is the most beautiful woman in the world. I am sexually attracted to my wife. This attraction is a biological good, since at least in principle having sexual intercourse with one's wife is the mode by which children are born. But human beings are not animals. My dog, Murphy, would enter a room containing food and consume the food immediately. He did not seek meaning in the act of eating. When he became sexually mature, he expressed his newfound desire by humping every single thing he could, dog or not. He was not concerned with moderation in eating or sex. He was an animal. Because human beings are not exclusively animals, our goal is to integrate our sexual desire into a higher norm—to let our sexual desire, which is part of being human, be directed toward the love of a particular person.

This healing of our sexual desire is how St. John Paul II defines *chastity*. Chastity is not a negative norm, a *no* to all sexual activity. Otherwise, chastity would be easy to accomplish since it would only necessitate avoiding sex. It might take a bit of work at the beginning. But as any mature married couple can testify, avoiding sex is a young man's struggle. As my marriage moves into its teenage years, I'm often more interested in consuming a glass of wine with my spouse or going to bed early than having sex. I guess that would mean that I'm chaste.

Not so fast! As St. John Paul II writes: "The full sense of the virtue of chastity cannot be fully comprehended without understanding love as the function of relating one person to another, the function disposed toward the union of persons."[7] Chastity means that the personalistic norm always interrupts and transfigures our sexual desire. Even a married couple, exclusively attached to one another, can be unchaste. Husbands and wives can forget about the person of their spouse, treating sex as nothing but an occasion for their own pleasure. Marriage does not grant a free sex pass where everything is permissible because now you're committed to one another. Marriage means that the real work of chastity begins.

And part of this chastity means that one considers one's spouse's pleasure as part of the sexual act. As we saw in chapter 1, hookup sex tends to be individualistic. It finds its highest form in pornography, where the individual experiences climax without another human being. In a chaste relationship, that's not possible. Part of marital chastity is being attentive to the reactions of one's partner in the sexual act. It demands willingness to engage in communication about sex itself, a topic that never ceases to be awkward even for the long-married couple. In a passage that many might find surprising, the future St. John Paul II writes:

From the viewpoint of loving another person, from the position of altruism, it must be required that the conjugal act should serve not merely to reach the climax of sexual arousal on one side, i.e., that of a man, but happen in harmony, not at the other person's expense, but with the person's involvement.[8]

To live chastely means to care about the mutual climaxing of man and woman in the sexual act. One cares about this not because the goal is to have really mind-blowing sex. Instead, chaste sex considers the good of our beloved before our own pleasure. Chaste sexuality within the marriage bond becomes part of the education into freedom and responsibility at the heart of human love.

For St. John Paul II, this is why contraception is a problem. Fertility (and even infertility) is part of the self-gift that a married couple offer to one another. My wife's personhood includes her identity as a woman. She is capable of having children. Receiving the gift of my wife, receiving her full personhood, means receiving her fertility as part of this gift. This doesn't mean that every couple must have fifteen children. Rather, it means that openness to life is one of the ways sex is ordered toward love of the concrete person before me. It also means that a husband cares enough about his wife's fertility that he does not view it apart from her whole personhood. Catholic husbands who treat their wives as pregnancy machines are as unchaste as those who use contraception.

The virtue of chastity is central for men and women who enter into the Sacrament of Marriage. We enter into married life as sexual creatures. Yet the salvific quality of marriage is that the powerful experience of our sexuality is taken up into a bigger story. The mature married couple can testify to this. Early in my relationship with my wife, I would have said that regular intercourse was central to our relationship. If we went too long without sex, I felt like we were missing out on something. With two kids to care for, this has changed. Rather, what is central to our marriage is now the deep and abiding love we have for one another. Our love is a deep companionship, a friendship, of which sex is only one part. Sexuality has been ordered to other acts of charity, like one spouse staying up all night with a sick child so that the other can sleep. It is not rare that when we do attempt to make love, one of the children will cry out or try to barge into our bedroom. Even when it is possible for us to engage in intercourse, one of us may come down with the cold or stomach bug that the children pass out like candy on Halloween. The virtue of chastity has enabled us not to resent the children, instead allowing the flowering of a rich bouquet of charity in our family. In other words, sometimes a backrub, a really good conversation, or a lazy Saturday spent playing with the kids actually allows a richer outpouring of married love than does sex. Remember, love is about communion, not about sex per se.

And that's why chastity, for those of us who are married, is actually a rather big deal. Chastity is the virtue that continually calls me to recognize my spouse as a person and not as a sexual object. Chastity is the virtue that opens the married couple up toward communion and helps us see every human being as gift rather than object. My formation in the virtue of chastity directly influences my ability to see my children as persons, my students as gifts rather than obstacles. Chastity heals us, restoring us as much as possible to the vocation of communion to which God called us.

The Soul Mate Theory Debunked

My concern in this book is the wounds that hookup culture inflicts upon men and women. Certainly this chapter's account of love as an unfolding drama, not a moment of sexual delight, offers a medicine to hooking up. In encountering our beloved as a human being worthy of love, we see the world anew. We come to truth. And we take up our roles in this drama, becoming lovers made for communion.

But this understanding of love is contradicted by another story about love, one that persists among both religious and nonreligious people: the story that every human must search the world for a soul mate.

There are all sorts of problems with this theory. First, it cannot explain the fact that we fall in love with lots of people in our lives. Kara was not my first girlfriend. She was not the first woman whom I loved. This does not mean that my earlier loves were simply a waste of time. Nor was I just eliminating possibilities. My earlier loves ended for a variety of reasons: I was not yet mature enough to make a commitment. The love that I offered was not returned. Each of these attachments provided an education in love, a formation for marriage that culminated in the relationship with my spouse.

Second, the theory of the soul mate turns love into fate. We cannot control fate; rather, fate just happens to us. A believer in fate would insist that it was my destiny to attend Notre Dame, where I would be happy and meet my spouse. If this person were a Christian, they would assert that God was pulling the strings of my heart so that I would meet my wife. Of course, this eliminates all human freedom. Yes, there is such a thing as divine providence, but it is a mystery. Often, we can perceive how God has acted in our lives only many years after the event. Turning love into fate would mean that God has abandoned those who don't find a spouse. It would mean that God intentionally has us fall in love, only for our spouse to get sick and to die. This is not the Christian God. God loves human beings; God is not some sadistic puppet master. God gives us people in our lives that we could date and marry. It is our responsibility to give our will over, to enter into the drama of love.

But those who do not discover their spouse immediately, those who suffer through a singleness they did not choose, are not casualties of a merciless system where there is only one person on earth they could marry. They didn't miss the boat because they were paying attention to other things. Divine providence for them means that if they gaze at their sorrow with the eyes of faith, they can see God drawing out of their suffering goods that they could never have imagined. As theologian Jessica Keating writes in a 2016 article about singleness in *America* magazine:

> No matter what shape or form my life takes—even if I don't marry until I am 75, even if I never marry—as a Christian I am called to the wasteful, uncalculating expenditure of love, a love that only flows from the open heart of Christ, a love that makes the in-between fruitful, that makes time abundant. It is the love that transforms the ambiguity of being single into the freedom of saying yes, "your will be done."[9]

Jessica is not a passive victim of never meeting her soul mate. She has entered into the drama of love with vigor. And through the gift of love that she has offered through her unexpected singleness, she has produced the richest of fruits in friendship, in mentoring, and in teaching.

Lastly, the soul mate theory erases the drama of marriage altogether. If Kara and I were soul mates from the beginning, if God pushed us together so that we would discover one another under the shadow of the Golden Dome, then do we actually love one another? Isn't the drama of love that I give my will to one other person, knowing full well that other people exist whom I could love? Marriage is not the discovery of some preexisting soul mate. It is a commitment to love this one person whom we are blessed to recognize as gift beyond gift.

In fact, the soul mate theory of love suffers from the same overly subjective approach to love that is operative in the hookup culture. What if, ten years into marriage, I met someone else and said to myself, "That's actually my soul mate." You hear this often from people who divorce their spouses: "I thought I loved you until I met him." "I thought you were perfect until I saw her." "I thought we would be together forever until things got difficult."

This account of love is deadly. It turns love into a detective game where we gradually uncover clues to the hidden plan of a devious God who brings people together only to rip them apart. The truth is that God did not create a *single* person for every one of us to marry. Instead, God made it possible for men and women to love one another, to commit totally to one other human being despite the unknown perils of the future.

Kara is not my soul mate because it was fate. Yes, God's providence brought us together—but then through a hidden grace (one that involved our own free cooperation), we made the decision to love one another forever. We could have married other people and been happy. But we didn't. And that's the gift of married love.

Conclusion

In this chapter, we have considered the nature of love as a dramatic communion of man and woman—a vision of love that is healing of the hookup culture. If men and women dared to love one another as persons, really sought out communion in the drama of love, this would be a healing balm for the wounds inflicted by hookup culture. We would not be afraid to share ourselves with another, and we would not rely solely upon the powerful feelings that sex brings out in us. We'd be committed to a self-giving love that relies on communion.

This natural love is not the exclusive property of Christians of course. Those who marry outside the Church can still serve as images of natural love for the world. But the Christian Sacrament of Marriage transfigures natural love, joining the communion of love shared between husband and wife to a different story entirely. Through the sacrament, the communion of husband and wife becomes a living sign of Christ's love for the Church, a sign of the communion of God with all humanity. If natural love provides a relief to the symptoms of hookup culture, the Sacrament of Marriage through communion provides a cure grounded in an encounter with Jesus Christ.

Exercises

1. This chapter describes love as a drama. Think about a relationship you've been in, past or present. How has falling in love been a revelation of truth for you? How did it transform your will? If you are currently in this relationship, tell your partner what you've learned about love.
2. Love involves both objective and subjective dimensions. The objective dimension is linked to recognition of your beloved's personhood, which makes it possible for you to see your beloved in a new light. How has the experience of loving another person objectively made you see that person anew? How did it heal your tendency to rely solely on your feelings in love?
3. Chastity is a central virtue for married love because it enables us to integrate our sexuality into a larger narrative. How has dating and/or marrying your beloved helped form you in the virtue of chastity? Where in your relationship do you need to work on your chastity? Ask forgiveness from your

girlfriend, boyfriend, fiancé(e), or spouse for any harm you have caused, and decide what concrete changes you will make in your behaviors. Make time to receive the Sacrament of Reconciliation, and ask forgiveness for your failures in cultivating this virtue.

4. **For Marriage Formation:** Marriage formation is necessarily human formation. What in this chapter gives you new insight into forming couples for married love? How might a program for marriage formation cultivate a deeper appreciation for the drama of love?

3.

Love's New Story

The church is filling up. Tuxedoed men greet guests in the back, stylishly ushering them to either the bride's or the groom's side of the church. Some of the guests are active Catholics—they know the drill. They genuflect as they reach their pews, lower their kneelers, and begin to pray. The college friends of the bride and groom have not entered a church in years. They remember the motions and try their best to fit in with the active Catholics. Other guests have no religious tradition at all. The beauty of the church building and the organ prelude filling the air captures the hearts and minds of the guests. As they catch sight of friends and family they haven't seen for years, they're distracted by the chance to catch up.

The bride and the groom met after college in Chicago at a local parish. One young adult night, they were placed at the same table, ironically for a talk on dating and marriage. They went out together afterward with a bunch of mutual friends and ended up speaking late into the night—too late for work the next day. At the end of the night, they exchanged numbers, and the groom-to-be promised he would call the next day. He didn't. In fact, he didn't call for three weeks. But he did call finally and ask his bride-to-be out on their first "official" date.

The date was nothing remarkable—dinner and a walk around the city. But they kept talking. And before anyone knew it, they had been talking and dating for six months. After six months, for some reason, the groom-to-be broke up with his bride-to-be. Neither dated anyone else—because after two weeks, the groom-to-be recognized the absurdity of his decision and came back with apology flowers, Cubs tickets, and a new awareness of the depth of his love.

Three months later, they were engaged. Wedding preparations commenced immediately as they secured the very church in Chicago where they first met. They went on a marriage retreat and met several times with a mentor couple. They scoured the city for a reception site for which one wouldn't need to take out a small business loan. Over the next six months, there followed cake tastings, shopping for dresses, wedding registries, flower shows, bridal showers, save-the-date cards, bachelor and bachelorette parties, ring shopping, invitations, assigning friends and family to tables for the reception, and on and on.

But the day is finally here. The bridesmaids join the tuxedoed gentlemen in the back of the church. Grandparents and parents process into the church first. Then come each bridesmaid and groomsman, followed by the maid of honor and the best man. And lastly, the bride herself.

The groom is already at the front, waiting for his bride. Although there is no church requirement to do so, they have decided they would not see each other before the wedding. Sure, it was superstition. But it was their freely chosen superstition. The bride is walked down the aisle by her father and mother, who both kiss her as she approaches the altar. She joins hands with her husband-to-be. They look overjoyed. At last, after a somewhat winding path, their two stories will merge into one.

God's Love Story

Few of us grow tired of listening to the love stories of family and friends. Children ask their parents to tell them how they met (parents often have to tell said story leaving out some of the details, of course). When friends become engaged, well-wishers don't just want to see the ring, they want to hear the play-by-play: where did it happen, and how did he ask? Many of our films, poems, and novels tell stories about falling in love. Stories about romance bring us to wonder, inviting us to stop and ponder the mystery of love through a particular account of affection.

From a Christian perspective, there is nothing wrong with attending to such stories of love. At weddings, people long to hear the couple's story of love recounted. They want to know about how the two met one another. They want to learn about the bride and groom's families. Such stories give us hope.

But such love stories are not enough to describe what is taking place at the wedding liturgy. Too often, I've attended weddings in which homilists describe the love of the couple without mentioning how this love will be transformed through their encounter with Jesus Christ's love. The priest offers a lengthy account of the couple's early years of dating. He describes the families of the bride and the groom, perhaps filling us in on the upbringing that formed the bride and groom into the people they are today. We learn about the couple's interests, their hobbies, their favorite sporting team, and where they plan to go on their honeymoon. Often enough, the priest canonizes the love of this couple—a unique love, the most wonderful love of all time.

But this approach does not attend to the greater story of divine love at the heart of the wedding liturgy. Yes, the natural love between husband and wife is necessary in the Sacrament of Marriage. There is an exchange of vows, a ceremony that alters the identity of both man and woman. The man becomes husband to this woman. The woman becomes wife to this man. There's something natural to this, linked to the order of creation. It's a big deal when men and women meet each other, fall in love, and pledge to live together forever and eventually form a family together. You don't need to be a Christian to imagine why human beings would figure out ways to mark this moment as solemn.

However, marriage in Catholicism is not linked only to creation. It's not merely natural. It is a sacrament, a sacred sign, that plunges us into God's history of working in the world. Our stories are written into God's history with men and women throughout time. As Joseph Ratzinger, later Pope Benedict XVI, writes:

> To receive the Christian sacraments means to enter into the history proceeding from Christ with the belief that this is the saving history that opens up to man the historical context that truly allows him to live and leads him into his true uniqueness—into the unity with God that is his eternal future.[1]

The couple entering into the bond of marriage are telling more than their own story, for the blessing of their vows is not just about them. Through the Sacrament of Marriage, they are remembering the story of love that God has enacted with humanity. Here, *remembering* doesn't mean recalling a fact or past event. It's a different kind of remembering in which the couple become a living sign of Christ's love for the Church. The Church "remembers" what God has accomplished through Jesus Christ by means of the vows the couple share with one another. By this sacramental remembering, the love of Christ for the Church is made present in a new way through the bond of marriage.

The transformation of the couple is by no means automatic. It requires that the couple realize what is taking place; they have to understand the story they are to become a part of. Their memories, their understanding, and their wills must be formed anew in the story of salvation. At the beginning of the marriage liturgy, after welcoming the couple and the assembly to the liturgy, the priest invites each person present to listen to the story of salvation that will unfold in the reading of sacred scripture that very day:

> Let us listen attentively with them [the couple]
> to the word of God that speaks to us today.
> Then, with holy Church,
> let us humbly pray to God the Father,
> through Christ our Lord,
> for this couple, his servants,
> that he lovingly accept them,
> bless them,
> and make them always one.[2]

More than the couple's particular love, the marriage liturgy celebrates the new creation that God is bringing about here and now. God reaches into the lives of men and women, into their stories of love and sin alike, and begins to write a new story from this day forward. From their encounter with the new story of love made possible through Christ, the couple can then offer their lives to one another. They can fulfill their calling to become this mystery of love in the world.

This new story is key to healing the effects of hookup culture. Even for couples with serious wounds from hooking up, the scriptures can serve as a healing medicine. In the scriptures of the Catholic wedding liturgy, we hear about a divine love that restores men and women to their original destiny as creatures made for self-gift. We discover a love made manifest in Christ, who did not objectify, did not control, but instead loved unto the very end. We see how married couples become signs of this love insofar as they enter into relationship with Jesus, who can heal our most grievous wounds. And we get a glimpse of the final moments of the story of God and humanity, the wedding feast of the Lamb that will spill over into all of creation. Ultimately, through the Bible, we learn that we are made for an even deeper communion with God.

A Nuptial Gloria

Marriage is a feast. We all know this intuitively. After the wedding ceremony, we pilgrimage to a reception site, where there will be food, drink, music, and dancing until late into the night. Jesus himself, along with his disciples and his mother, attended a wedding at Cana where they ran out of wine!

But the marriage liturgy itself is a feast, before we even get to the reception. We know this because the Church's festive song, the *Gloria in excelsis* ("Glory to God in the highest") must be sung during the wedding Mass. If the marriage takes place during Advent or Lent, when the *Gloria* is typically not sung, there still has to be a *Gloria*!

The *Gloria* orients us to listening to the scriptures during the wedding liturgy. Often, the telling of a story is simply the explication of a series of events that happened once upon a time. When my wife's paternal family gets together for a wedding or a funeral, many stories are told. They remember holiday gatherings at the family-owned funeral parlor where all major feasts were celebrated. They remember moments in which children got into trouble. The stories often last so long, become so central to the gathering, that you forget why you got together in the first place.

In the *Gloria*'s first line, we hear why Christian story telling is different: "Glory to God in the highest, and on earth peace to people of good will." This first line of the *Gloria*, taken from the Gospel of Luke, proclaims Christ's coming among us at Christmas. At every Mass where we sing the *Gloria*, we become participants in the drama of the Incarnation—the Word becomes flesh and dwells among us anew. Christmas did not just happen once upon a time. It is the feast where God entered fully into history, casting his lot with us, never leaving again. As we sing at the Vigil Mass on Christmas from the prophet Isaiah, "The glory of the LORD shall be revealed, / and all flesh shall see it together" (Is 40:5). God's glory has been revealed in the birth of the Word made flesh, power made perfect in weakness. Our resurrected Lord remains flesh, now married to the Church. That's the meaning of the feast of the Ascension. When we read the scriptures, we're not just telling a story from the past. We're recalling the meaning of the present.

As the couple and assembly listen to the Word of God, they're listening to the only story that can make sense of the present. In a particular way, the couple is hearing how God is about to make new their story of love. They should assume a posture not merely of careful listening but of longing for God to act here and now.

One of the possible readings for the wedding liturgy is from the Song of Songs. This book of the Bible operates at a variety of levels. It tells the story of a bride, betrothed but still awaiting the wedding feast, who is longing to unite fully with her bridegroom. This is what the Church calls the *literal* sense of the scripture. The Song of Songs also provides an image for us of the love between Christ and the Church: Jesus is the Bridegroom and the Church is the Bride. This is the *allegorical* or metaphorical sense. We are to see a story of God's relationship with each and every soul. God longs to be united with us. This is the *moral* sense. Lastly, there is a sense of the scriptures that is anagogical. This is the mystical interpretation, a foretaste of our experience of union with God. Attending to each of these senses of the reading can help us to assume the proper disposition while listening to the scriptures, not just at a wedding but always.

The Song of Songs begins with the bride calling out, "Let him kiss me with kisses of his mouth, / for your love is better than wine, / better than the fragrance of your perfumes. / Your name is a flowing perfume" (Sg 1:2–3). Taking up the literal sense, whenever we are apart from our beloved, it is only natural that we long to hear their voice, to hear their name. We long to touch our lips to theirs, to once again enjoy their presence. The couple entering into the Sacrament of Marriage know this desire. They have longed for their wedding day, and at last it is here.

But, the scriptures don't just have a literal sense. In its allegorical sense, the Song of Songs makes clear that listening to the scriptures in the nuptial liturgy should not be like sitting in a waiting room: Yes, I'm here for a really important appointment. Yes, I'm waiting. So, I'll just flip through the pages of this random magazine to keep me busy before the real event.

No! In the scriptures, we hear about God's insatiable desire for us. Jesus Christ is the Bridegroom, who longs to be united to his Bride. And the entire Church assumes the role of the Bride in longing to hear the name of our beloved uttered in our midst: Jesus Christ, the Word made flesh. We sing to him in the *Gloria*, offering our voices as instruments expressing our desire: "You alone are the Holy One, you alone are the Lord, you alone are the Most High, Jesus Christ . . ." Every one of our desires is met in the Word made flesh, in the splendor of the Father, in Jesus the Bridegroom.

This encounter with Jesus in the scriptures changes us. There is always a change of heart, a moral conversion that comes when we encounter Jesus in the scriptures. St. Bernard of Clairvaux writes about the moral dimension of this kiss of Jesus Christ given through the scriptures:

> To you, Lord Jesus, how truly my heart has said: "My face looks to you. Lord I do seek your face." In the dawn you brought me proof of our love, in my first approach to kiss your revered feet you forgave my evil ways as I lay in the dust. . . . [I]n the kiss of the hand, you imparted the grace to live rightly. And now what remains, O good Jesus, except that . . . you would graciously bestow on me the kiss of your mouth, and give me unbounded joy in your presence.[3]

This is the very posture, both exterior and interior, we should assume as we listen to the Word of God at the wedding liturgy. Some of us, including the couple themselves, need to experience the Word of God as a healing kiss, one that can forgive the sins we have committed, those times when we have loved poorly. This Word comes to us in the scriptures as sweet medicine, forcing us to examine whether we have loved our spouse-to-be as Christ loves the Church. Have we used them sexually? Have we failed to acknowledge our beloved as the gift that they are? Have we ordered our relationship toward the worship of God? The readings during the nuptial Mass foster in us a change of heart, one that comes as through a kiss.

Many who listen to these scriptures will hear in them reflections of the graciousness of God in our relationship. We have received the "kiss of the hand" that imparts to us the grace of daily living out rightly the mundane nature of married life. Such moments may not seem like occasions for divine desire. We put children to sleep. We pick them up from school. We eat and pray together as a family at night. We attend Mass together on Sundays. Yet in each of these moments, the Bridegroom comes to dwell among us, to kiss us with wisdom and grace. As the long-married couple listens to the scriptures, they discover anew the mystery of love at the heart of their existence, something they can easily forget.

And lastly, every one of us should long for the final kiss, the kiss that is total union with God. This is what we mean by the "anagogical" sense. The kiss that the married couple will share this very day is a visible sign of that eternal kiss. As we contemplate the love of husband and wife, realized in this bride and this groom, we recognize God's total longing for us. We prepare for our moment of consummation with God each and every time we open our ears to listen to the divine Word—God's nuptial speech echoing through the ages.

The Nuptial Imagination

There are many different readings to choose from for the celebration of a Catholic wedding.[4] One should choose an Old Testament reading, a Responsorial Psalm, a New Testament epistle (letter), and a Gospel text. During the Easter season, the first reading should be from the book of Revelation, rather than from the Old Testament. If one is married on a Sunday or another holy day (where marriages are allowed on such days), one should use the readings of the day, replacing one with one of the scriptures about marriage.

Those preparing for marriage should immerse themselves in the biblical texts available for the liturgy, readying themselves to hear the Word of God on their wedding day. At first, this immersion may be focused more on choosing the texts to be read at their wedding. Once the texts are chosen, the couple should enter regularly into prayer around them, reading them together at least once a week. Those who are already married can find in these texts a deep treasury of memory, an infinite storehouse for contemplating the gift of nuptial life.

We can identify four threads in the readings for a wedding Mass that are worth contemplating in light of the theme of this book: marriage as a medicine for hookup culture. These themes are (1) the re-creation of man and woman in the image and likeness of God, (2) the revelation of Jesus Christ as Bridegroom of the Church, (3) the participation of husband and wife in the nuptial love of Christ, and (4) the wedding feast of the Lamb.

1. Re-creation in the Image and Likeness of God

From the very beginning, human beings were made for communion. In an act of love, God created man and woman as oriented toward communion with each other and creation. In Genesis, there are two accounts of the creation of Adam and Eve. In the first, man and woman are created as the culmination of the sixth day of creation:

> Then God said: Let us make human beings in our image, after our likeness. Let them have dominion over the fish of the sea, the birds of the air, the tame animals, all the wild animals, and all the creatures that crawl on the earth.

> God created mankind in his image;
>   in the image of God he created them;
>   male and female he created them.

> God blessed them and God said to them: Be fertile and multiply; fill the earth and subdue it. (Gn 1:26–28a)

Both man and woman are created in the image and likeness of God. This likeness is not a matter of physical resemblance, since God is neither male nor female. Instead, human beings are created like God for self-giving. The God who created the world as an act of love invites men and women to share in this generous love. Through their fertility, man and woman share in God's own creativity.

The second account of creation in Genesis 2 is earthier. Adam is created from the very dust of the earth. God's breath fills Adam, bestowing life to this earth-creature. Filled with God's Spirit, Adam is oriented toward self-giving love, abiding in perfect harmony in paradise. God invites Adam to share in the process of naming creation, allowing him to participate in God's creativity. But among all the creatures of the earth, Adam does not find a companion. Thus, God performs the first surgery, wounding Adam so that he might heal him:

> So the LORD God cast a deep sleep on the man, and while he was asleep, he took out one of his ribs and closed up its place with flesh. The LORD God then built the rib that he had taken from the man into a woman. When he brought her to the man, the man said:
>
> > "This one, at last, is bone of my bones
> > and flesh of my flesh;
> > This one shall be called 'woman,'
> > for out of man this one has been taken."
> > (Gn 2:21–23)

At last, Adam has found a companion among all the creatures. He was created with God's very breath, but only when man meets woman, when Adam recognizes the union he is meant to share with Eve, can he express the fullness of the divine life he is called to. Marriage is not a creation of the Church. Instead, it is a primordial sacrament through which men and women become, in St. John Paul II's words, "a visible sign of the economy of truth and love, which has its source in God himself and which was revealed already in the mystery of creation."[5] By "economy," the Church means the way God has arranged the household of the world. In the love of husband and wife, we see that God has oriented the world toward communion. The relationship between man and woman, their orientation toward self-gift, and their capacity to bring new life into the world show forth the graced nature of creation itself.

But we're not in paradise anymore. The sin of Adam and Eve is a refusal to participate in this economy of self-giving love. Eve takes the fruit from the tree of the knowledge of good and evil , in the process demonstrating her doubt in the goodness of God's existence. God has given everything to man and woman. Yet Eve grasps rather than receives. Adam, refusing to believe in the possibility of forgiveness, eats the fruit with her. His heart is closed to the mercy of God. It is Adam who announces the damning effect of their anticommunion: when asked by God why he ate from the forbidden tree, why he could not be obedient to the simplest of laws, Adam responds, "'The woman whom you put here with me—she gave me fruit from the tree, so I ate it'" (Gn 3:12). Adam blames both God and his wife. And in doing so, he introduces a new wound into the communion of paradise: man and woman, rather than participating in the economy of divine gift giving, now operate in an economy of scarcity, an economy of the will to power—may the strongest win.

We see the effect of this economy in the hookup culture. A young man does not receive his beloved as gift but instead uses her, subverts her very humanity, by masturbating to pornographic images. Both man and woman cut off communication, engaging in sexual intimacy but refusing to share the desires of their hearts with one another. Husbands and wives leave one another when it becomes too difficult to keep their commitment, when desires shift, often casting blame on the other for declining passion in love. The failure to communicate in love is a loss of communion.

The Word became flesh to heal men and women of this loss of communion. The Word became flesh to restore us to our original destiny as creatures meant to love God and neighbor. When Jesus Christ ascends the mountaintop to preach to his disciples in the Sermon on the Mount, interpreting the Law in a new way, he draws us into the economy of salvation made possible by the kingdom of heaven. This kingdom of heaven is made present in his very person. He preaches the Beatitudes, giving us the great charter of this kingdom in which we learn that humility, mercy, purity of heart, and meekness must be some of the virtues of its citizens. We discover that the very heart of the law is total love, a total gift of oneself to the logic of gift in each of the commandments:

> You have heard that it was said, "You shall not commit adultery." But I say to you, everyone who looks at a woman with lust has already committed adultery with her in his heart. . . . It was also said, "Whoever divorces his wife must give her a bill of divorce." But I say to you, whoever divorces his wife (unless the marriage is unlawful) causes her to commit adultery, and whoever marries a divorced woman commits adultery. (Mt 5:27–28, 31–32)

Love demands more than the bare minimum. Divine love makes possible restoration to the original harmony in creation, a return to our vocation as created in the image and likeness of God.

Jesus Christ comes to manifest to us what it means to be created in the image and likeness of God. He proclaims to us that to be truly human means to take up one's cross and follow in the footsteps of the beloved Son. In marriage, we perform this discipleship by becoming like little children who love with fidelity, commitment, and trust. In marriage, man and woman are re-created in God's image and likeness. Their bond of love cannot be broken, cannot be ripped apart: "'What God has joined together, no human being must separate'" (Mt 19:6). We have been created for communion with God and one another. Through the Sacrament of Marriage, we experience anew this communion of love.

In this sense, our love of our spouse, our commitment to their well-being, our fidelity to their flourishing, is not just a matter of having a healthy marriage. The deeper the communion we share with our spouse, the more we reflect the original destiny of creation. We are made for love, and marriage can become an image of paradise on earth.

2. Christ as Bridegroom, Church as Bride

Israel saw her relationship with God as analogous to marriage. This was a stunning claim. Many religions saw sex as integral to religious practice, but few applied the image of marital love to the covenant between God and people.

God is faithful to Israel as a husband is faithful to his bride. And Israel must offer the gift of her total love in return: obedience to the commandments through worshipping God and loving one's neighbor. Israel struggled with such spousal love. She cheated on God by entering into covenants with other nations, with other gods. She defrauded the poor, desecrated the Temple, and forgot the original encounter of love when God fed her with manna from heaven. She struggled to be God's people, to offer her will in total love.

Yet God, the creator of the world, promises to redeem Israel through a new covenant, one that will never end. If Israel cannot love sufficiently on her own, God will provide the capacity to love:

> See, days are coming—oracle of the LORD—when I will make a new covenant with the house of Israel and the house of Judah. It will not be like the covenant I made with their ancestors the day I took them by the hand to lead them out of the

land of Egypt. . . . But this is the covenant I will make with the house of Israel after those days—oracle of the LORD. I will place my law within them, and write it upon their hearts; I will be their God, and they shall be my people. They will no longer teach their friends and relatives, "Know the LORD!" (Jer 31:31–32a, 33–34a)

God's writing of the divine law upon the human heart will mean that the return gift of love will become nearly automatic. Our whole selves will be so aligned with the divine will that we love God with ease. In the same way that husband and wife often complete one another's sentences, Israel and God will perfectly know each other's minds. The nuptial covenant between God and Israel will last forever. All of Israel will become an extended wedding feast: "For the LORD delights in you, and your land shall be espoused" (Is 62:4b).

This expectation that God would come to enact a new covenant, to begin the final stages of the wedding feast between God and Israel, is fulfilled in the New Testament. In the Gospel of John, we discover that the new covenant has indeed been written upon the human heart, enshrined in the heart of the Word made flesh (see Jn 1:14). In the Gospel of John, the first miraculous sign accomplished by Jesus is at the wedding at Cana. Jesus, his disciples, and his mother attend a wedding, an event that would last nearly seven days. But the unimaginable happens: the hosts run out of wine.

Jesus' mother, Mary, asks her son to intervene in the matter, but he replies, "'Woman, how does your concern affect me? My hour has not yet come'" (Jn 2:4). In the Gospel of John, the "hour" of Jesus is his ultimate manifestation of glory upon the Cross, when all the nations learn the depth of divine love. Although his hour has not arrived, Jesus relents and performs a sign that points to this hour:

> Now there were six stone water jars there for Jewish cere-
> monial washings, each holding twenty to thirty gallons. Jesus
> told them, "Fill the jars with water." So they filled them to the
> brim. Then he told them, "Draw some out now and take it
> to the headwaiter." So they took it. And when the headwait-
> er tasted the water that had become wine, without knowing
> where it came from, . . . the headwaiter called the bridegroom
> and said to him, "Everyone serves good wine first, and then
> when people have drunk freely, an inferior one; but you have
> kept the good wine until now." (Jn 2:6–10)

The six stone water jars serve as an image of creation awaiting
completion on the seventh day. Such jars would have held a very
large quantity of water, likely twenty to thirty gallons each. Jesus
provides abundant wine for the celebration. The choicest of
wines has been served in the final days. Jesus is the bridegroom
whose glory is revealed at a wedding to show that his hour is at
hand. Through Christ's action, marriage becomes a sign of the
feast of the kingdom of God.

In the Gospel of John, the culminating moment of this feast
is revealed on the Cross. The hearty imbibing of the copious
wine of the kingdom at the wedding at Cana becomes the sparse
sipping of sour wine by our crucified Lord:

> After this, aware that everything was now finished, in order
> that the scripture might be fulfilled, Jesus said, "I thirst."
> There was a vessel filled with common wine. So they put
> a sponge soaked in wine on a sprig of hyssop and put it up
> to his mouth. When Jesus had taken the wine, he said, "It is
> finished." And bowing his head, he handed over the spirit.
> (Jn 19:28–30)

The hour has finally come for the wedding feast of the Word
made flesh. It is the Crucifixion, when love shines into the dark-
ness of death and conquers it. And from the side of our crucified Lord come blood and water—signs of both Baptism and

Eucharist, the sacraments through which one enters the Church. Even this event is related to a wedding. The Greek word for "side" (pleura) in the Gospel of John is taken from the word for "side" (pleuran) in the second creation account in Genesis in the Greek translation of the Old Testament, the Septuagint. Just as Eve came forth from the side of Adam, so now the Church as the Bride of Christ comes forth from the side of the Bridegroom. In the Gospel of John, the Crucifixion, the moment in which Jesus Christ reveals the depth of divine love, is also the wedding day for the Church.

For this reason, every wedding is an occasion to consider anew the sacrificial love of Christ the Bridegroom. Human love finds in the sacrificial love of the God-man its new standard. But this love is not merely about suffering; it is the gift of God's entire self to humanity. It is a love that seeks to redeem every dimension of human love. As Pope Benedict XVI writes about divine love:

> The love-story between God and man consists in the very fact that this communion of will increases in a communion of thought and sentiment, and thus our will and God's will increasingly coincide: God's will is no longer for me an alien will, something imposed on me from without by the commandments, but it is now my own will, based on the realization that God is in fact more deeply present to me than I am to myself. Then self-abandonment to God increases and God becomes our joy.[6]

The exchange of love between husband and wife, an exchange of wills that forever makes them one, gives us an image of this divine love to contemplate. Husband and wife make us aware of the possibility that our will can be united, not simply to another person, but to God. The scriptures paint for us an image of salvation as a wedding feast of self-giving love. And thus every human act of self-giving love, especially in marriage, recalls to us this glorious, divine economy of salvation.

3. Marriage as Participation in Christ's Love

Few readings elicit more sideways glances at weddings than Ephesians 5:2a, 21–33. In this passage, St. Paul exhorts the Christian married couples of Ephesus to see in the union of Christ and the Church the basis for their own marriages. St. Paul reminds wives to submit to their husbands in imitation of the Church's own submission to our Lord. Likewise, he instructs husbands to love their wives as Christ loved the Church. Each time my wife and I hear this reading at Mass, we playfully glance at one another when the reader proclaims our respective exhortations.

The language of submission is not popular with my students. After all, what precisely does submission consist of? In our fallen world, does this call to submission become an excuse for misuse of power, wherein a husband seeks to control his wife? Couldn't the adoring love of a wife open her up to violence at the hand of her husband? Aren't St. Paul's exhortations limited to the time in which he was writing, one in which the wife was dependent on her husband in order to survive? Can't we just dismiss his message?

While these objections to the passage are understandable, they miss its point entirely. St. Paul's message is actually countercultural, grounding the love of husband and wife not merely in the fallen world of sin but in the mystery of Christ's love. Husband and wife alike are to offer their submission first and foremost to Jesus Christ: "Live in love, as Christ loved us and handed himself over for us. . . . Be subordinate to one another out of reverence for Christ" (Eph 5:2a, 21). The language of subordination and submission recalls Israel's submission to the

Law in the Old Testament. In the New Testament, both husband and wife are to "submit" their wills to one another just as
Christ handed himself over for the life of the Church. Through
the mystery of Christ's self-giving love on the Cross, the relationship between husband and wife is forever transformed.

The wife becomes an image of the Church in relation to
Christ. The Church does not submit herself to Christ as if he is
her overlord, demanding from her the destruction of her will.
Rather, Christ is so closely linked to the Church that although
he cannot be collapsed into the Church, he is totally united to
her: "For the husband is head of his wife just as Christ is head
of the Church, he himself the savior of the body" (Eph 5:23).
Here, we may have objections. In my own marriage, I do not
exercise headship over my wife, if by headship we mean that I
dictate to her what she'll wear, how she'll organize her day, or
what career she'll take up. To do so would be, once again, to
miss the point. For Paul, the husband—who did exercise such
headship over his wife in the ancient world—could not exercise
it in a domineering way. Instead, his headship was to be like
Christ's, a headship of total, self-giving love.

Husband and wife together share in the mystery of redemption. Christ's spousal love has touched the very heart of human
love, transforming married love so that it might become a sign
of the union of Christ and the Church. This transformation is
a moral one that is to alter every dimension of the couple's love.
As St. John Paul II reminds us, "Marriage corresponds to the
vocation of Christians only when it reflects the love which Christ
the Bridegroom gives to the Church, his Bride, and which the
Church . . . attempts to return to Christ."[7] Husband and wife
must constantly attune themselves to the mystery at the heart of
their relationship, the love of Christ and the Church. In other
words, they have to give up the temptation to make love about
power and control. Love is gift.

No couple enters this mystery of divine love overnight. Husband and wife live into it, discovering new resources for incarnating divine love as they pilgrimage through life. This need for constant attunement is why 1 Corinthians 13 is so widely chosen for weddings even though it does not address marriage at all. The passage is preceded by the image of the Church as Christ's very Body. St. Paul is writing this letter to the Church in Corinth partially in response to abuses of eucharistic practice in which hierarchies of power have been set up in the Church. The rich have been bringing a meal to enjoy before the eucharistic banquet, sharing none with the poor. Members of the community are competing over which charisms of the Spirit each has received. There's a fight in Corinth over who has the power.

Paul responds by reminding the Church in Corinth that each member of Christ's Body has its function, none more important than the others. He writes that the only way the Church can live her deepest identity as a community of men and women gathered in Christ's sacrificial love is to adopt this love as their own:

> Love is patient, love is kind. It is not jealous, [love] is not pompous, it is not inflated, it is not rude, it does not seek its own interests, it is not quick-tempered, it does not brood over injury, it does not rejoice over wrongdoing but rejoices with the truth. It bears all things, believes all things, hopes all things, endures all things. Love never fails. (1 Cor 13:4–8a)

This way of living love is the vocation of each and every person in the Church, married or not. But a married couple has a particular vocation to live out the deepest identity of the Church in their relationship. The mystery of their love is taken up into the love of Christ for the Church. Husbands and wives are not always patient with one another or with their children. They do not always bear burdens with love. But as the couple enters further into the nuptial mystery of the Church, they will learn to participate more fully in Christ's love for the Church.

For this reason, it is important that the wedding homily not merely be a laudatory account of the couple's current love. Instead, the homilist must set in front of the couple and all those gathered with them the total, self-giving love of Christ. The couple need to see the horizon of what is possible in loving one another. They should be challenged to contemplate Christ's love, to use his love as a measure of their own love. The homilist should bring up the possibility of real difficulties in marriage, for the nuptial love of husband and wife is not merely some ideal expressed only in pious thoughts. It is the conforming of every dimension of their relationship to the mystery of love hidden in Christ. For in loving our spouse as Christ loved the Church, we discover anew the love of God: "Beloved, if God so loved us, we also must love one another. No one has ever seen God. Yet, if we love one another, God remains in us, and his love is brought to perfection in us" (1 Jn 4:11–12).

4. The Wedding Feast of the Lamb

The Bible ends with a wedding in the book of Revelation. Few couples think about including this apocalyptic text at their wedding liturgy. After all, isn't the book of Revelation about a weird vision of what God will do in the future? Isn't it about predicting the end of the world? Who wants to hear about this during a wedding?

Yet this is a misunderstanding of the book of Revelation. Apocalyptic literature in the Old and New Testaments imagines God's final judgment of history. Right now, we see violence all around us, but there will come a time when the final judgment will unfold, when God will console the faithful, bringing them to the fullness of eternal life.

The text from Revelation for the wedding liturgy deals with the final moments of history. God's reign has been established, destroying the violence on earth, and the heavenly hosts cry out, "'Let us rejoice and be glad / and give him glory. / For the wedding day of the Lamb has come, / his bride has made herself ready. . . . Blessed are those who have been called to the wedding feast of the Lamb'" (Rv 19:7, 9). The final image from the book of Revelation is of the city of God descending on the earth, transforming every dimension of creation into a wedding feast. The violence and power of this age cannot conquer the love of God that descends from on high.

This seems a rather dramatic vision to connect to an ordinary wedding of man and woman. Yes, we are celebrating a wedding feast. Yes, many of the guests do feel blessed to be invited. But is our marriage really an image of the final judgment of God upon history?

The answer, of course, is yes. In the marriage of man and woman in Christ, the harmony and peace that God intended for creation is reestablished. Man and woman receive an image of the final destiny they were created for: the wedding feast of the Lamb. This vision is to become the calling of the couple. Their home becomes a space where every dimension of creation is acknowledged for its destiny of eternal life with God. Their daily meals become occasions for communion with one another. Their raising of children becomes an image of the communion of love that governs the New Jerusalem, the redeemed city of God.

Striving to become an image of heaven itself is at the heart of the nuptial mystery of the Church. The couple, in exchanging vows, commit themselves to living this mystery. Thus, they must hear through the scriptures this story of salvation again and again, discovering their deepest identity as living signs of Christ's love for the world—living signs that breathe a bit of eternity, a bit of heaven itself, wherever they go.

Conclusion

Through immersing their imaginations in the scriptural narrative, the couple and the rest of the wedding assembly form a
new understanding of married love. They come to the church
building with a story of love, but surely that story is not all good
news. Perhaps there have been times when they have failed to
love one another. They may have understood love as a matter
of grasping power. In this they are no different from the rest of
humanity, prone to choose power and prestige over the deeper
communion of self-giving love made possible through the power
of God's love.

The scriptures heal the couple and the entire assembly,
enabling them to think about love anew. The scriptures give us
a new horizon for what is possible in marriage. We discover a
love that is about communion rather than power. We discover
that the mystery of marriage is grounded in the love of Christ
for the Church, a redemption that restores man and woman
in some way to a heavenly love. This redemption of love is not
automatic, but will take a lifetime of uniting the personal story
of our love with God's love, made manifest in the scriptures.

Thus, the Bible provides a balm for hookup culture that is
far more powerful than exhortations against unmarried sex: It
shows us that human beings are made for total communion with
God. It shows us how the love of man and woman can reflect
God's love for humanity. And it trains us to comprehend that
the mundane love of husband and wife reflects a mystery more
wondrous than eye can see.

As the wedding Mass continues, the couple will do more
than reflect on this story of love. They'll enact it with their very
bodies.

Exercises

1. During the next thirty days, pray with the readings for the Celebration of Christian Marriage alone, with your boyfriend or girlfriend, with your fiancé(e), or with your spouse. (You can find these texts here: http://www.foryourmarriage. org/catholic-marriage/planning-a-catholic-wedding/readings/). What have you learned about God's love through praying with these texts? What have you learned about how your own love story reflects God's?

2. The desire to seize power rather than give oneself away is the opposite of love. How do you see yourself opposed to love? How do you seek out power in your relationship rather than giving of yourself? Write a prayer to Christ the Bridegroom, asking for healing grace. Pray this prayer over the next three months.

3. Every marriage is oriented toward eternity. Talk with your boyfriend or girlfriend, your fiancé(e), or your spouse about your marriage. Where do you see a glimpse of heaven in your relationship? Where do you struggle to see it? What might you do to manifest the heavenly wedding feast more clearly in your day-to-day life? For example, you may set Sunday aside as a time to spend together in prayer, conversation, and friendship.

4. **For Marriage Formation:** As with every sacrament, there is a kerygma, or proclamation of the Good News, in marriage. The kerygma in marriage is grounded in the love of Christ the Bridegroom for his Bride, the Church. How could you include dimensions of this kerygma more regularly in a marriage formation program? Read Leonard J. DeLorenzo's book *Witness: Learning to Tell the Stories of Grace That Illumine Our Lives* (Notre Dame, IN: Ave Maria Press, 2016). How might you compose witness talks around the Sacrament of

Marriage that take seriously the nuptial story found in the scriptures?

4.

Be Mine

The moment is finally here. The bridal party stands at the front of the church, ready to witness the marriage vows. The priest approaches the couple and asks them to hold hands. He reads some words, to which almost no one is paying attention. Everyone is looking at the bride and the groom, who are overflowing with nervous delight.

The whole Rite of Marriage takes no more than fifteen minutes. Promises that include love until death are made with surprising ease. There might be a tear or two from the bride and groom, the parents might be a hot mess, but it's all over quickly. Everyone resumes their places in the pews, and the gifts are brought forward just as they are during a normal Mass.

Fast-forward three years to a flurry of evening activity. The wife, a doctor at a local hospital, has just wrapped up a twelve-hour shift that began at five o'clock in the morning. The husband arrived home earlier after finishing up a day of teaching eleventh-grade social studies. On the way home, he picked up their year-and-a-half-old son from day care. He has cooked dinner, watered the plants, and sung "Row, Row, Row Your Boat" sixty times. When his wife walks in, she beholds a disaster area. Angry that his dad is attending to something as mundane as dinner rather than playing a game with him, their beloved child has thrown every one of his toys around the house. There is wailing and gnashing of teeth on the part of dad and son alike.

The young family quickly consumes dinner. Mom rushes her son upstairs for a bath, while Dad does the dishes and cleans up the explosion of toys. Then the husband begins the routine of putting the son to bed, a task (including three stories followed by a nighttime prayer) that normally consumes close to an hour and a half. The grading that must be accomplished goes undone another day. His wife goes downstairs to pay the bills. Around nine thirty, the spouses join one another in bed, where they manage to exchange a couple of words before falling asleep.

Their son comes out of his room in distress at ten forty-five. He has vomited up dinner, somehow getting it on every wall in his room. The room and the child must be cleansed anew. The wife does not work the next day, so she spends the next six hours comforting her son as he suffers through a surprise stomach bug. Both husband and wife know that the illness that has taken over their son's body will find a way into their systems tomorrow. Until then, there is work to do and a child to care for.

Yet somehow they're not entirely miserable. They find a way to laugh with one another about their son's ability to cover a whole room with vomit. Though they know that the inevitable spread of this illness will bring yet more chaos into their already difficult-to-manage lives, echoing in their minds are the words they uttered in their act of consent on that special day only three years prior:

> I, N., take you, N., for my lawful wife/husband,
> to have and to hold, from this day forward,
> for better, for worse,

for richer, for poorer,
in sickness and in health,
to love and to cherish
until death do us part.[1]

The Act of Consent

In chapter 1, we discovered that one of the many problems with hookup culture is that it forms men and women who are incapable of making a lifetime commitment to one another. They grow to see the relationship between man and woman as akin to a process of exchange. Since relationships exist to make me feel good about myself, when I no longer feel good, then it's time to leave. Transaction complete.

Yet at the heart of the Church's Rite of Marriage is a promise of faithful permanence, a promise that I'll let this communion with this person guide every aspect of my life as long as we're both alive. The couple ministers the Rite of Marriage to each other through their vows, the act of mutual consent to marriage that expresses this commitment:

> A Marriage is established by the conjugal covenant, that is, the irrevocable consent of both spouses, by which they freely give themselves to each other and accept each other. Moreover, this singular union of a man and a woman requires, and the good of the children demands, the complete fidelity of the spouses and the indissoluble unity of the bond.[2]

In both the early and medieval Church, the act of consent was not necessarily given before a minister. The original celebrations of marriage were Masses, offered in thanksgiving for the union of husband and wife that took place as late as thirty days after the couple made their vows to each other. Because of the need to determine the validity of consent—to make sure that the couple really intended to come together forever—this act of consent was eventually taken up into the Church's official liturgy.

The domestic origin of the act of consent helps to explain why its wording does not mention God. The husband and wife do not call upon God to sanctify their union. They have listened to the scriptures. They have heard the words of the priest telling them of the gravity of their action. But marriage at its center is about a mutual submission of wills, an offering of permanent, lifelong commitment to one's spouse.

Many couples coming to the Church for marriage are surprised to find out that they cannot write their own vows. These couples have learned about marriage vows through film and television weddings where husband and wife compose their own vows. These vows may mention the moment that the couple fell in love. They may describe the permanence of the nuptial union in metaphoric language: I love you more deeply than the deepest sea. Such particular expressions of love are, of course, good. We want couples to communicate their affection to one another. But the set vows offered in the nuptial liturgy do not depend on the subjective feelings of the couple. The consent is given as an objective fact, a sober commitment of the man and woman to each other.

Before they offer their vows, the priest asks the couple three questions to verify their willingness to enter into the Sacrament of Marriage. Responding to the first question, they promise that they have come to the Church freely. If either of the two is only getting married because they have been coerced, forced into the union by circumstances beyond their control, then they cannot make a free act of consent. Love requires a sober freedom, a wholehearted commitment to love this particular person. Second, the priest asks the couple if they are prepared to enter into marriage as a lifelong commitment. Lifelong fidelity is a good of marriage, enabling love to flourish because each spouse knows that the other will never leave except through death. Lastly, the couple promises to be open to the birth of children (a question that can be omitted if the couple is beyond child-bearing age) and to raise them in the life of the Church. This openness to life is intrinsic to marriage, which is between men and women who are sexual beings. Sex is not just for the couple's personal satisfaction; it is the way children are born. Openness to life, to welcoming children into the nuptial mystery, is evidence that the couple really intends to be married.

Marriage in the Roman Catholic Church is an exchange of consent that presumes what we've called natural love. This natural love becomes conjugal, creates a bond, in the permanent consent offered before a minister of the Church. The act of sexual union, what the Church calls *consummation*, solidifies these vows. The intimate gift to each other of the husband's and wife's sexuality after their exchange of consent is a bodily performance of what they have promised.

Even at the natural level, the act of consent is healing of hookup culture and the wounds it causes to men and women. It is a moment of profound communication, one in which husband and wife pledge to spend the rest of their lives together. This vow makes possible an intimacy that surpasses sexual pleasure. Sexual activity becomes an embodied commitment to the other person that takes place within a broader relationship in which there are other goods, such as procreation, lifelong fidelity, and an indissoluble bond that allows love to flourish. This natural dimension of marriage—including the commitment—fosters the flourishing of society itself, as children can be born into a union in which they discover the fruits of love.

The consent offered in marriage extends throughout the life of the couple. The moment of consent orders the relationship between man and wife: they are to love one another forever. The commitment to this love does not come from interior disposition alone; it is upheld by the laws of state and Church alike. Every moment the couple remains faithful to their vows, loving one another in sickness and in health, the act of consent is renewed.

Consent as Consecration

But the act of consent between a baptized woman and a baptized man joins them in a way that transcends the natural state of marriage. Something else happens in the nuptial consent of two Christians in the Church. From the moment of consent, their relationship becomes ordered to a new reality: they become signs of God's communion with the human race.

How is this possible? Baptism forever changes us. When we are baptized into the name of the Father, the Son, and the Holy Spirit, we receive what the Church calls a new *character*. This character has often been described as a spiritual mark or seal upon the Christian that changes our identity. The German theologian Matthias Scheeben describes character as that which brings us into a particularly intimate connection with Jesus. He writes that the character imprinted upon us in the Sacraments of Baptism, Confirmation, and Holy Orders "brings us into contact with Christ as the source of grace, as the heavenly vine whose branches we are through the character, and . . . gives us a right . . . to possess grace if we set up no impediment to it."[3] The character of Baptism and Confirmation bestows on us a deeper relationship with Christ; our identities become intimately united to Jesus Christ, so that the Spirit of our risen Lord dwells in our hearts. Nothing can erase this character or remove it from our identities. Our whole selves become ordered to divine worship. In both Baptism and Confirmation, we receive a character that marks us as Christians, as those made to proclaim to the world that Jesus is Lord. The divine gift of love pulsates through us, making this work possible. We only need to cooperate.

It is the divine grace of Baptism that brings the couple into a unity of wills, for baptized Christians are always priests, prophets, and kings or queens. In marrying one another, husband and wife are exercising their priesthood by consecrating their love to the triune God, a consecration made possible through Christ's presence in them. They are prophets, testifying to the world that God is love. And they are royal figures who come to rule over the created world in the context of their service to the domestic church, a reign that brings about the peace of God's kingdom.

So when two baptized and confirmed Catholics stand before the priest and offer consent, they do so through the Spirit of Jesus that is their deepest identity. As Scheeben comments on the Sacrament of Marriage:

> When a Christian man and woman contract marriage they enter into a closer union with the God-man as the bridegroom of the Church who abounds in grace. He Himself receives them and consecrates them as active organs in His mystical body. . . . [B]y reason of their new rank, new grace and new life must flow into them from the source of the head. This is chiefly an increase of sanctifying grace, but it also involves a right to all the actual graces they need in their new state for the fulfillment of their sublime duties.[4]

The couple offers the vows of marriage not merely through the wills of each individual, but through the will of Christ, which is part of who they are. The baptized couple becomes a living sign of Christ and the Church through each person's complete self-gift to the other. No couple could do this on its own; it is Jesus Christ who makes this offering possible.

The *sanctifying grace* the couple receives in the sacrament is a permanent transformation in the couple's act of self-gift. The bond of love that unites the couple is suffused with grace, with the Spirit of Christ. Every act of love the couple shares, including their sexual love, is taken up into the economy of God's love.

Actual grace refers to the concrete gifts of love bestowed by God in the day-to-day work of living out their life together. Christ has consecrated their relationship to himself, and now God, who is love, pours out gift upon gift on the couple. All they must do is receive this love. St. Thomas Aquinas thus refers to the Sacrament of Marriage as offering something like a "quasi-character."

The sacrament brings a deepening of the couple's relationship with Christ, a closer communion with the nuptial mystery of the Church. The sanctification that takes place in Christian marriage extends far beyond the moment of consent. Marriage brings about a permanent, ongoing transformation of the identity of the couple. Their married life, with all of its joys and sorrows, conveys grace to the world. And the love they share with one another increasingly becomes an image of the love of Christ and the Church. As Cardinal Marc Ouellet writes:

> As a charism that consecrates the couple to Christ, the marriage bond causes them, and their conjugal love in all its dimensions, to participate in Christ's love for the Church. The sanctification of the spouses, founded on baptism and marriage, will increase to the extent that they live out the charism that has made them "one flesh," a task requiring their openness to the particular graces that heal, purify, perfect, and even divinize their love.[5]

Through the mundane acts of love that the couple carries out in family life, man and woman, as well as the entire world, are sanctified in Christ.

This is a stunning claim! The households of most married couples would seem to an outside observer to be rather boring places. If you listened in on one of our family dinners, you'd hear each of us recount our days. You'd hear our son describe in his five-year-old way what he'd like to do that evening. There would be bottles made for a baby, coffee prepared for the following morning, and baths given to children. All of this seems so normal. But through the vows of love that we have shared before God and the Church, my wife and I are actually sanctifying all of creation by doing stuff that seems so normal. Through our communion of love, we transform creation into a space where divine love can be found.

For Catholics, this is why the act of consent is so important. It is not just an expression of feelings at a particular moment and a promise to give this marriage a good try. Rather in the Catholic Rite of Marriage, consent is a new consecration to Christ. Divine love now circulates between the baptized spouses until the separation of death. Marriage is indissoluble for Catholics not because the Church disagrees with divorce but because the bond of love that unites husband and wife together is Christ's love for the Church.

The mystery of marriage is that the gift of love offered in the wedding liturgy is only the beginning. The couple learn to love one another with divine love through the day-to-day work of paying the bills, caring for a home, raising children, going on dates with one another, emptying the dishwasher, sharing sexual intimacy, and simply being present to one another in good times and in bad. Husband and wife alike encounter the mystery of Jesus Christ through such commonplace activities.

The act of consent shared by husband and wife is no ordinary promise. It is akin to the moment of Baptism when the human being enters into a new relationship with the triune God. It is akin to the Eucharist, when bread and wine are transubstantiated, consecrated, into Christ's Body and Blood. The love of husband and wife is sanctified, transformed in order to become an image of Christ and the Church. That's why the priest at the wedding liturgy says these words after the couple's consent:

> May the Lord in his kindness strengthen the consent
> you have declared before the Church,

and graciously bring to fulfillment his blessing within you.
What God joins together, let no one put asunder.[6]

Their whole lives now become a wedding liturgy where the mystery of divine life breathes through their fidelity, their openness to life, and the indissoluble bond they share.

Bad Times

Lest one overly romanticize what unfolds in marriage, it is necessary to recognize that this act of consent can go wrong. The couple promise to love one another "in good times and in bad, in sickness and in health . . . all the days of my life."[7] There will be bad times. Husband and wife may lose their jobs, leading to a financial crisis that stresses both the couple and their children. There will be both physical and mental illness that complicate the promise of love unto the end of life. Miscarriages may wound the hearts of husband and wife so deeply that they find it difficult to express in words, even to one another.

The worst difficulties in marriage, though, are often self-imposed. Husbands and wives cheat on one another, making it difficult for one partner to offer the return gift of love. Some spouses just leave when it gets too difficult. There is domestic violence that places both husband and wife, as well as their children, in physical danger. Alcoholism and other addictions can ruin relationships as one spouse or both refuse to face how addiction is ruining family life.

In many of these instances, the marital relationship cannot continue. Sometimes this means that husband and wife must live apart from one another for days, weeks, or even years. Sometimes, it means that husband and wife will have to face the possibility that they were incapable of authentic freedom, of giving full consent to marriage. It may come to light that the husband had been cheating on his wife well before the wedding. The Church may discover that the wife was an alcoholic even while they were dating, that her will had been given not to her spouse but to drink. It may be the case that husband or wife never intended to love the other forever, having professed to a friend before the wedding that there are always "starter marriages." A deeper analysis of a situation of domestic violence may reveal that the husband never intended to love his spouse with his whole being but rather sought to manipulate and control her. In such instances, one spouse may pursue an annulment of the marriage. This isn't Catholic divorce. It is rather a recognition that full consent could not be given—that the permanent nuptial bond was never present.

Nonetheless, the Church teaches that in most cases, even in the midst of some of these difficulties, the nuptial bond remains present. Husband and wife really did vow their lives to one another, fully aware of what they were doing. Falling out of passionate love is not a sufficient reason for an annulment. The vocation of husband and wife in such instances is to transfigure the suffering through love, to accompany one's spouse toward healing. Such acts of love may not be successful. One's husband or wife may still be withdrawn, an absentee spouse and parent, more concerned with his or her work than with the marriage. Undoubtedly, this produces sorrow on the part of the faithful spouse. Yet, in loving one's spouse even when the return gift is not perceivable, the faithful spouse transforms suffering into an act of love. As Dietrich von Hildebrand reminds us:

> Through Christ, suffering has acquired an entirely new meaning. What was merely an inexorable *consequence* of original sin before Christ has now assumed the character of a fruitful *penance* and *purification*—a manifestation of love. Suffering love has redeemed the world. The cross stands forth as the

symbol of redemptive and expiatory suffering freely accepted by merciful charity.[8]

We should not seek out this patient suffering in our marriages, entering into marriage with someone because they're hard to deal with. We should strive for the kind of love described in chapter 2. But when such self-giving love is not perceptible to the married couple, they can't just give up. Instead, they take the diminishment of love, the sorrow that wounds their hearts, and offer it back to the Father in love. In this self-sacrificing, they participate in a real way in the life, death, and resurrection of Jesus Christ (what the Church calls the Paschal Mystery).

This participation of the couple in the Paschal Mystery of Jesus Christ shows how God is saving the world through the ongoing act of nuptial consent. As I tell my undergraduates, it's kind of a big deal. That's why I also tell them that they should memorize these vows—not just because it's impressive to speak them from memory at the altar, but because these vows should become part of their day-to-day married lives. They should recall them regularly on anniversaries, as well as during moments of joy and crisis. Their children ought to grow up hearing these vows, knowing that the source of their parents' love is this act of consent, which has changed history itself.

Sacramental Signs of Consent: Rings, *Arras*, and Sex

Sacraments work through the language of signs. In Baptism, the sign is water. In Confirmation, it is sacred chrism. In the Eucharist, it is Christ's Body and Blood. In marriage, the sign is the consent of the couple. But we cannot see or touch the act of consent the way we can see and touch water, oil, bread, and wine. Therefore, there are "sacramental" signs intended to bring to mind the reality of this consent for the couple. First, the couple is invited to exchange rings. The exchange of rings is an ancient practice linked to the bestowal of wedding gifts by husband and wife. Rings become a tangible sign of the permanence of consent. Rings are precious and hard to dissolve or destroy. They're so solid that they conform our bodies to their shape: my wedding ring has reshaped my left ring finger, leaving a permanent mark upon my body. As Andrew says in St. John Paul II's drama *The Jeweler's Shop*:

> The rings in the window
> appealed to us with a strange force.
> Now they are just artifacts of metal,
> but it will be so only until that moment
> when I put one of them on Teresa's finger,
> and she puts the other on mine.
> From then on they will mark our fate.
> They will constantly act as a reminder of the past,
> as a lesson to be memorized for good,
> and they will constantly open up the future,
> joining the past to the future.[9]

In addition to serving as a sign of indissoluble natural love between the couple, the rings draw the couple toward the source and summit of their love—the Holy Trinity. The man and woman put rings on each other's hands, saying, "N., receive this ring as a sign of my love and fidelity. In the name of the Father, and of the Son, and of the Holy Spirit."[10] Invoking the Holy Trinity is more than pious practice. It is a challenge for the couple to let the measure of their love be God's own eternal, begetting, and fruitful love. When I look down on my ring, it should become for me a mirror. Do I pray for my spouse? Do I see her as Christ does? Have I been a husband and father who has received divine love so that I can give it away? Have I shared the gift of my love with the world, becoming a sign of

Christ's love in the classroom and the city? The ring's reshaping of my finger makes it clear that this commitment to divine love comes at a cost. It is an ongoing sacrifice, necessitating not only an abstract commitment to self-gift but the participation of my very body.

The wedding liturgy may also include the giving of *arras*, simple gold coins that are also linked to the traditional exchange of gifts in the act of consent. The blessing and giving of the *arras* entered into the Church's liturgy through a medieval Spanish liturgical rite (the Mozarabic) and is thus very common in places throughout the world that were colonized by Spain. The minister blesses the coins, saying "Bless, O Lord, these *arras* that N. and N. will give to each other and pour over them the abundance of your good gifts."[11] The bride and groom then share the coins with one another, praying that they may become a promise of God's own blessing and a sign of the gifts of marriage.

Like the rings, the coins function at both a natural and a supernatural level. Naturally, money is a gift to the couple. Money means that they will be able to enjoy feasts with each other, to have a large family if possible, and to share a whole life together in the world. Money is connected to engagement with society, to participation in the social order. The couple's relationship will unfold through the renewal of this social order as they bring children (who will cost money) into the world. But there's a deeper meaning to the exchange of coins as well. God, the giver of all good gifts, has performed an act of hospitality in creating and redeeming the world. This act of hospitality extends to the couple, who have entered into the order of gift giving that is God's very life. In the exchange of coins, they pledge to one another that their lives will become an image of the coins, an icon of a hospitality that shares everything with their children, with the poor, and with the lonely. The family itself will become a space of divine hospitality.

The practice of exchanging *arras* calls to mind my parish in Newton, Massachusetts. Peg and Bill LaRoche welcomed Kara and me, a young couple who had just moved to the area, into their home. Bill would always attend our youth group's work camp, sleeping on the ground next to kids fifty years younger than he. Peg urged him to do this, to give back some of the gifts they had received. Every holiday, they invited anyone and everyone into their home. On Christmas Eve, they had a party. On Easter, a dinner. Every Sunday, everyone was welcome to stop by for a drink and a chat. The LaRoches' hospitality formed my wife and me to reimagine the meaning of nuptial love. It is not the private sharing of life together, a love that cares only for the beloved, but a love that opens up to the world, extending God's hospitality to everyone.

The last sign of consent is married sex. Happily for the guests, this sign is not present in the current marriage liturgy itself. While we do want to see the act of consent, it's best of course to let consummation be a private act. But medieval Christians handled this sign differently: they processed from the church to the bride and groom's home to witness a blessing of the couple's bed given while the newlyweds were *in it*! These Christians understood that sex, the act of consummation, was part of the marriage liturgy. In married sex, the couple enacts what the spouses promise—the gift of their very bodies to one another, a total union of will, and bodily desire. Contemporary moral theologian John Grabowski goes so far as to call the act of sex in marriage a sacramental remembering of the covenant of love between husband and wife and thus Christ and the Church:

> [M]arital sex is genuinely sacramental—that is, it is integral to the sacrament itself as the completion and recollection of the consent that causes it. This is true not only of the first time a marriage is consummated—as a narrow reading of canon law might suggest—but of all of the conjugal acts that

make up the sexual communion of a couple. These too recall and in fact make present the grace that a couple's consent conferred on them. They thus participate in the marriage bond that unites a man and a woman as "one flesh" over the whole of their lives.[12]

Marital sex is a recollection of the total, self-giving love that the couple has committed to. They become one flesh in sexual union, a bodily sign of their deepest identity. The result of this union is children, manifesting to the couple that their love is to be fertile, giving new life to the world.

This sacramental account of intercourse in marriage is healing of the act of sex. For those reared in the creeds of hookup culture, sex is not a sign of anything at all. It is meant purely for pleasure, for enjoyment, for the sake of the orgasm alone. Those who have learned to have and understand sex in this way enter into marriage requiring healing. They need to discover a much broader and deeper meaning of sex, one that is not reducible to pleasure. Married sex, as Grabowski describes it, locates the deepest meaning of the act of intercourse in the Sacrament of Marriage itself. We are made to give ourselves away entirely in love. Sexual union in marriage is not the end, or goal, of nuptial love but a sign that points us toward its proper end: total self-gift. Sex points toward communion.

The act of consent in the Sacrament of Marriage is about a deepening of communion. In the hookup, sex and love are separated. Sacramental marriage not only unites sex and love through the communion of husband and wife, but it goes further, inviting the couple to see their love as participating in God's own communion. Because Christian spouses are oriented toward communion, communication—including around sexual issues— is part of Christian marriage.

Married sex in the Christian economy is not reducible to mind-blowing, out-of-body experiences of total ecstasy. In reality it's often mundane. It is practiced by those who raise kids all day, who work full-time jobs, and who have but a moment to delight in one another's presence. Married sex will be interrupted again and again by illnesses, children struggling to fall asleep, travel, and general exhaustion. The irony is that marriage changes the meaning of sex. Intercourse between husband and wife exists within a much larger narrative, a story in which husband and wife are to become an image of Christ and the Church. That's the heart and meaning of marriage. Sex serves as a sign of this meaning, but it's one sign in a larger complex of signs including taking out the trash, cleaning up vomit, and going on a date. Because of the sacramental transformation that takes place, everything in marriage becomes a sign of divine love.

Conclusion

At the end of the Catholic marriage rites, a hymn or song of praise is to be sung by the assembly.[13] Singing is a sign of joy, celebration, and festivity. It is only right and just that the assembly sings a song of praise having witnessed the transformation of this man and this woman into husband and wife. But singing is not an act of efficiency. The Department of Motor Vehicles does not chant its driver's test. The university does not produce its paperwork in hymn form. Singing points toward something greater than efficiency. We sing because what has taken place in this union of husband and wife is greater than the completing of a process. It is the beginning of a new drama, a loving commitment that has the power to transfigure the world.

If the philosopher Josef Pieper is right to say that only the lover sings, then those who have encountered an icon of Christ's very love are compelled to sing. And this song accompanies the couple along the way, not just to the reception site, but to the eucharistic banquet, where they will learn over the course of a lifetime what it means to love one another as Christ loves the Church.

Exercises

1. In journaling or in conversation with a friend, your boyfriend or girlfriend, your fiancé(e), or your spouse, discuss how indissoluble commitment would help you love someone more. What would or does make this commitment difficult for you?
2. The vows made in the marriage liturgy are an act of consent that continues throughout the marriage. What does this mean for the day-to-day living of married life? What practices would you need to embrace in order to nurture fruitful married love?
3. If you're married, memorize the consent for marriage (wedding vows) and use this as a prayer together once a week. Reflect on how you might live these vows more fully. If you arcn't married, memorize these vows without saying the name of your beloved (remember, consent is a really big deal!). Pray once a week that you will receive the grace to live out these vows in your life.
4. In marriage, sex is to be a sign of the act of consent, the commitment to total and absolute self-giving love. If you are married, where in your relationship does sex function in this way? Where doesn't it? What practices would you need to take up for sex to become a sign of nuptial love? If you aren't married, how do you understand sex? Do you see it as a sign of something more or just an expression of physical delight? What would need to change for you to see sex as an icon of married love?
5. **For Marriage Formation:** If marriage formation is to do anything, it should prepare couples to speak their vows

to one another with full, conscious, and active participation. How does your marriage formation program do this? How might you change your program to focus on the speaking of these vows not simply as a natural act of love but as a supernatural one, transforming the couple into a sign of Christ and the Church? What practices would you suggest that couples take up to make this transformation fruitful?

5.

Lift Up Your Hearts

We stood in the entryway to Our Lady of Fatima church, surrounding my grandmother's ashes. Present were my wife, my children, my mother and father, my brother, and my grandfather beloved husband to Margaret Thompson. My grandfather, physically weak, greeted the guests who came to pay their respects to Peggy. Peggy had died after a decade-long battle with Alzheimer's. She had spent the last days of her life in my parents' home in hospice care after a series of strokes in the previous months took away the last vestiges of both her physical capacities and her memory.

Grandma and Grandpa met in Jersey City, New Jersey, when her brother introduced the two of them. They married in 1956, neither having completed high school, and by 1957, my mother was born. They then moved to Florida along with other family members. Their marriage was not always easy—the good ones never are. After we lost our biological father, early in our lives, they helped to raise my brother and me. From their love, I learned about sacrifice. I learned about commitment. I discovered what friendship could look like in married life. It was my grandmother who taught me my prayers, who insisted that even though I did not participate in the first year of religious education at my parish in Florida, I would receive First Communion during second grade. My grandparents passed on to me the gift of faith and thus, in some sense, my career.

My grandparents loved one another with a love that matured even as Alzheimer's began to wreak havoc on my grandmother's nervous system. They still went out together to the local Cracker Barrel at least three times per week, ordered their water with lemon, and basked in each other's presence. They were proud of their daughter and their son-in-law. They loved their grandchildren. They adored their great-grandchildren. In the last years of her life, my grandmother rarely made it to the church. She couldn't go out for very long. Plus, it was painful, I suspect, to have to explain to well-known friends what was happening to her. It was a steady reminder to both my grandparents of the end of their lives. It was too much.

Yet here we were once more, processing down the aisle of Our Lady of Fatima to sit in the front pew. Once again, my grandfather celebrated the Eucharist with his family. This time, his wife was no longer among the living.

My grandmother didn't dictate a lot about her funeral. She simply demanded Mass—she wanted to be remembered in the eucharistic liturgy of the Church. And she wanted Schubert's "Ave Maria" sung, because this piece had been sung at her and my grandfather's wedding. As my wife sang the "Ave Maria," as tears flowed from our eyes, I couldn't help but recognize the fittingness of this moment. When my grandparents had declared their love for one another in the Sacrament of Marriage, they had promised to be present to one another until death. In between, they had lived their marriage (not always perfectly) as a eucharistic mystery. Their attendance at Our Lady of Fatima, their holding of hands throughout the liturgy, renewed their bond of nuptial love week after week. As my grandfather said goodbye to his wife, praying that she might now join the nuptial liturgy of heaven, he once more received Christ's sacrificial love in the Eucharist. In the closing moments of her life, he had promised that he would keep her memory alive as long as he lived. He fulfilled his promise in the liturgy this day, in the reception of Christ's Body and Blood.

When the liturgy was over, the family processed out the back doors of the church and stopped before the columbarium right outside the church where my grandmother's ashes would be laid to rest. A plaque on the columbarium lists my grandparents' names. In parentheses are their dates of birth, as well as my grandmother's date of death. One day, the family will return to Our Lady of Fatima to celebrate the funeral rite once more, this time for my grandfather. His date of death will be engraved on the plaque to mark his entry into eternal rest alongside his spouse. And we will continue to remember both of them in the eucharistic liturgy of the Church, to pray that the eucharistic life of love they shared with one another will have led them to the nuptial feast that never ends.

The Eucharist as a Renewal of Vows

The Rite of Marriage and the Mass are closely linked to one another. If two baptized Catholics are married, then the celebration of Mass is not just optional. It's required unless there is a good reason to not celebrate Mass (perhaps the couple knows no Catholics, and it would be awkward to have sixty guests fumble their way through the Mass).

But *why* is the Mass normally required for the weddings of baptized Catholics? Because our celebration of the Eucharist is always a festive remembering of the wedding of Christ and the

Church. The great mystic and Doctor of the Church St. Hildegard of Bingen describes the Mass as a wedding feast in which the Eucharist itself is the wedding gift offered by God to the Church: "When Jesus Christ, the true Son of God, hung on the tree of His Passion, the Church, joined to him in the secret mysteries of Heaven, was dowered with His crimson blood; as she herself shows when she often approaches the altar and reclaims her wedding gift."[1] The blood of Christ spilled on the Cross functions as a sign of the totality of divine love. In Jesus Christ, God has offered the fullness of himself to humanity. Christ's act of self-giving love, as we saw in chapter 3, was the wedding day of the Church—the moment in which Christ became the Bridegroom of the Church. The Eucharist, insofar as it is a sacrament of this sacrifice, is for St. Hildegard the wedding gift offered to us by our noble Bridegroom. To receive the Eucharist is to enter into the marriage of Jesus and the Church.

One of the prefaces to the Eucharistic Prayer for the wedding liturgy makes the link between marriage and the Mass explicit. It reads, "In the union of husband and wife you give a sign of Christ's loving gift of grace, so that the Sacrament we celebrate might draw us back more deeply into the wondrous design of your love."[2] The language of the prayer is intentionally ambiguous. Is it talking about the Sacrament of the Eucharist, or the Sacrament of Marriage? Actually, it's both! The marriage of husband and wife becomes a sign of the covenant of love that God has offered to humanity. Husband and wife become a sign of Christ's love for the Church. To spend time in their presence should be to discover anew the mystery of divine love, the presence of Christ's sacrificial love now permeating existence. The Eucharist plays precisely this role in the life of the Church, in the life of the entire world. As twentieth-century mystic Adrienne von Speyr writes about the Mass:

The gesture of sacrifice now embraces everything. Our personal sacrifice cannot be distinguished from the sacrifice of the Church, which, in turn, is indistinguishable from the sacrifice of Christ that resides in the Father's sacrifice to the world. And the Eucharist is all of this: the sacrifice of the Church with all her members, the sacrifice of Christ and the sacrifice of the Father who gave his Son to die on the Cross for all humanity.[3]

Our celebration of the Eucharist transforms creation into a space where the divine sacrifice of love is poured out again and again for humanity. The newly married couple is called to this same sacrifice of love.

Thus, every time the couple celebrates the mystery of the Eucharist, they are renewed in their own nuptial love. One could think of regular eucharistic participation by the couple as a daily or weekly renewal of their marital vows. When the couple prays the Eucharistic Prayer with the Church and receives Christ's Body and Blood, their charism of eucharistic charity is restored. Sometimes, the couple may not sense this restoration. They may be fighting with one another. They may be bringing a small gaggle of children to Mass, unable to concentrate on what is happening during Mass. But their very reception of divine love, whether they feel it or not, brings them back into the mystery they have become in marriage: a sacrifice of love for the world.

This is why the Eucharist is obligatory in the nuptial liturgy for baptized Catholics beginning their lives together as one body, brought together through Christ's love. They consume the Bread of Life so that their home might become a space where divine love is present to all. They drink of the chalice of salvation so that their love may spill over in charity. Their calling is from the beginning a eucharistic one, grounded in the mystery of sacrificial love. They will live out this mystery in often-mundane family life, transforming creation in the process.

The requirement that the couple marry within the celebration of the Eucharist heals them of an assumption that they might have been operating under: the assumption that their marriage is all about them. It would only be natural for them to assume this. They have been the focus of attention while they proclaimed their vows to one another. They're the ones wearing the tuxedo and the fancy dress. Against this temptation to self-centeredness, the eucharistic liturgy becomes for the couple a lifelong reminder that they have been married in order to become a sign of divine love for the world. Their marriage is for the salvation of themselves, but also of their children and of the entire world. Their communion is for the world!

It was only through regular eucharistic practice that I came to discover this truth. At first, I saw the pain of infertility as a burden given exclusively to us.[4] It was our terrible cross, the suffering that inflicted itself on our marriage. I was miserable in my suffering, and yet I also grew to love it. It became my personal cross that only I could understand. I could not even share it with my wife. But weekly participation in the Eucharist broke me of my selfishness. Even infertility could become for us a gift, bringing us to take up the vocation of adopting parents. Out of our sorrow, we could make a space for love, for a form of sacrificial love that led to greater communion in the world.

The Eucharist thus bestows a pattern on the couple. Their lives are not their own. Their marriage is not about personal fulfillment. Instead, the Mass teaches the married couple that love increases only when it is given away.

The Nuptial Blessing

At a wedding Mass, the Liturgy of the Eucharist unfolds, for the most part, as one would expect. But immediately after the Our Father, additional rites enter in. Once again, a rite originating in

Spanish liturgical custom is allowed in the United States when suitable: the blessing and placing of the *lazo* (a rope that ties the couple together) or a veil. The couple kneel before the eucharistic presence of our Lord and are joined together, the *lazo* or veil becoming a sign of the bond that has brought them together.

Then, the Nuptial Blessing is said over the bride and bridegroom. Before the Second Vatican Council, this prayer was a blessing only for the woman.[5] After the council, new prayers were written so that the blessing would be offered over the bride and the groom together.

The structure of the Nuptial Blessing is similar to that of other blessing texts used by the Church, including the Blessing over Baptismal Water. The prayer begins through remembering what has been accomplished through the union of husband and wife in the divine plan of salvation. The Church then asks that the Spirit might descend anew on the couple, strengthening their sacramental union. Specific blessings are given to each spouse, that they might be able to fulfill their vocations as husband and wife, father and mother. The prayer concludes by asking that God might lead them to the heavenly banquet.

The prayer is beautiful, helping to form the newlyweds' understanding of their vocation as a married couple in the world. It reminds them that they have been created in the image and likeness of God for a communion of personhood that is a sign of God's own love. They are living symbols of the mystical marriage of Christ and the Church, serving as mirrors to the Church of the nuptial love at the heart of her existence, a living memory of what Christ has accomplished in the created order.

Yet they must live into their identity as made for divine love. The prayer asks that the Spirit of the Father and the Son might descend on them to become what they have received in the sacrament: "Graciously stretch out your right hand over these your servants (N. and N.), we pray, and pour into their hearts the power of the Holy Spirit."[6] This calling down of the Holy Spirit upon the couple is called an *epiclesis* (meaning in Greek a "calling down"). Of course, the couple has already received the Spirit in Baptism—it was the Spirit that made possible the speaking of the vows in the first place. But now a fresh outpouring of the Spirit is given, one that is to remain with the couple for the rest of their days. Like the Virgin Mary, they have given their consent to God, their "May it be done to me," so that they might be a fruitful sign of divine life. The prayer continues, asking that the couple "may share with one another the gifts of your love and, by being for each other a sign of your presence, become one heart and one mind."[7] This cannot be accomplished by the human will alone. It is the work of God that so transforms married life.

In this sense, every couple should be aware that their love for one another is pure gift. Too often, happy marriages are seen as a form of "works righteousness," where couples that are blessed with happy unions are lauded for their virtue. Christian marriage is not an achievement, even if it does take real work. Couples who experience blessing in their marriage should recognize it, constantly returning to the eucharistic altar to give thanks to God for the mystery of love that envelops them.

The Nuptial Blessing reminds the couple that sex is procreative as well as unitive. In their love, expressed through sex, they become a sign of Christ and the Church. But to become this sign they must, like the Church, be open to fertility. Such fertility is ordered toward the creation of a home, a space where divine love dwells. This expanding notion of fertility calls the family to look outside of itself, to recognize that the love the family has received is meant to be given away: Pope Francis writes that "even large families are called to make their mark on society, finding other expressions of fruitfulness that in some way prolong the love that sustains them."[8] Yes, fertility is essential to living out the liturgy of marriage in the world. Yes, the most basic form of this fertility is the gift of children. But this fertility will take different forms, bestowing divine life on the cosmos even if the couple cannot have children for whatever reason.

For most couples, children are part of this blessing. Catholic couples should want to have children. They should want to form a home, a space where love dwells. The Nuptial Blessing reads, "May they also sustain, O Lord, by their deeds the home they are forming and prepare their children to become members of your heavenly household by raising them in the way of the Gospel."[9] Like God's love, the love of husband and wife is oriented toward generosity. The gift of children is the manner in which God allows the couple to share in the mystery of divine creativity. As Pope Francis writes in *The Joy of Love:*

> The gift of a new child, entrusted by the Lord to a father and a mother, begins with acceptance, continues with life-long protection, and has as its final goal the joy of eternal life. By serenely contemplating the ultimate fulfillment of each human person, parents will be even more aware of the precious gift entrusted to them. For God allows parents to choose the name by which he himself will call their child for eternity.[10]

For the wife, this means that her very body enters into the mystery of life as divine love is poured out through her pregnancy. Her joy and very real suffering through pregnancy become a participation in God's own love.[11] For the husband, whose body is not as directly affected, this means that he must take up his role as father. Fatherhood means assuming a responsibility that extends beyond biological requirement to become a gift of self to one's beloved child.

This last point is an important one for those who are unable to have children. Parenthood is more than a merely biological activity, for children always come to us as gift; this is a truth that

infertile couples realize quickly.[12] Adopting children is still an act
of divine creativity. Adoption is "not merely a pale and blood-
less copy of real fatherhood, but . . . can be a means of grace,
destined to make up for the deficiencies of biological filiation."[13]
Biological parenthood can operate as mere obligation, simply a
way for the species to reproduce itself. But adoption, in Catholic
theology, becomes an image of the authentic gift of parenthood.
We do not grasp after fatherhood or motherhood. But we pray
for it in the Nuptial Blessing because it comes to us as total gift.

Parenthood thus flows from the divine love at the heart of
the Sacrament of Marriage. The fact that children are a gift does
not mean that every couple *must* have a large family. A couple
may determine that it is not the right time to have more children, because of their cultural, financial, or social situation and
remain open to the gift of life while also planning their family
responsibly. This too is an act of divine creativity, of graciously
receiving the gift of one's procreative capacity.

Lastly, the Nuptial Blessing reminds the couple of their ultimate destiny—eternal life with God: "Grant, holy Father, that,
desiring to approach your table as a couple joined in Marriage
in your presence, they may one day have the joy of taking part
in your great banquet in heaven."[14] A great blessing of marriage
and family life is that it becomes an education into longing for
heaven. Neither spouse will live forever on earth. The destiny
of each spouse is to enjoy unity with God forever and ever, what
the Church calls the *beatific vision*.

Does this mean that there is no marriage in heaven? Too
often, this question is answered in a lazy way. At one level, no,
there is no marriage in heaven. Sacraments are for living human
beings. And the sign of divine love that a married man and
woman represent will not be needed in heaven, where the fullness of this love will be available for the contemplation of all.
But at another level, a couple's marriage does not disappear as

they pass into eternal life. For marriage forms the Christian in the art of self-giving love, giving one practice for the eternal enjoyment of God. We learn to see in our spouse, in our children, in family life itself, a vision of the wedding feast of the Lamb. When we participate in this wedding feast in eternal life, how will we not see glimpses of our spousal love? How will we not hear hints of our children's playful voices in the singing of the angelic hosts? We won't forget our beloved in heaven, but will remember them all the more. The more we love our spouse and children here, and the more we strive to see them through the lens of eternity, the more we'll be able to recognize the meaning of the wedding feast of the Lamb in every dimension of our lives.

The Family as Eucharistic Icon: Memory, Sacrifice, and Communion

St. John Paul II writes that "the essence and role of the family are in the final analysis specified by love. Hence the family has the mission to guard, reveal, and communicate love, and this is a living reflection of and a real sharing in God's love for humanity and the love of Christ the Lord for the Church his bride."[15] The family becomes an icon of the Church, of the love of Christ dwelling among mortals. It does so through sustaining memory, teaching sacrifice, and bringing each person into communion. In this sense, we can think about each and every family as having a vocation drawn from the Eucharist itself. The family is an "icon" or image of the Eucharist!

The family is a setting for remembering what God has accomplished in Christ. Husband and wife discover in their children images of divine grace. My own children have become for me icons of Christian joy, making me aware of the wonders of Christmas and Easter, of the beauty of incense, and of the power of Jesus' love to transform even the youngest heart. We pray together as a family, kissing icons, singing hymns of joy, and interceding before God for one another. We light Advent wreath candles and celebrate saints' feast days together. We stop regularly at the Grotto at the University of Notre Dame, lighting candles for my students, for our beloved dead, for all those who are lonely. In the context of the family, remembering what God has accomplished through Christ is not a matter of rote memory, but a living memory, warming our hearts to adore the living God. In the context of the family, the memory of salvation is alive and well, made available for the world to see.

The family is also a place where Christian sacrifice is taught. If the heart of the family is the eucharistic mystery of the self-giving love of Jesus Christ, the family lives out this sacrificial gift from day to day. I'll always remember the transition that took place when my wife and I brought our son home from the hospital. During the first seven years of our marriage, everything had been about us. We ate together in peace. We slept together through the night. We traveled where we wanted. We often went on dates. But our son called us toward a new form of love that was not only about us. We learned to sacrifice, to give ourselves away to this child that depended entirely on us. Tranquil meals, long nights of sleep, exotic trips, and frequent dates ceased. We found ourselves catching vomit in our hands, spending wakeful nights worrying about fevers, and long days childproofing our home. Surprisingly, we found that there was nothing more delightful than this sacrifice of love in which we were being formed.

When we brought our daughter home, we saw how this sacrifice of love extended out from us to our son. For the first time, our son learned that he was not the center of the universe. He learned to worry about her crying, her fragility, saying gently,

"Don't worry, my Maggie, it will be okay." He discovered the need to (sometimes) share his toys, his parents, and his very life with his sister. The family learns the sacrifice of the Christian life through the gift of day-to-day life together. This life isn't perfect. As Catholic writer Anna Keating notes, "We need to rediscover that life lived in relationship is not about perfection but about faithfulness."[16] Fidelity in a fallen world is always a sacrifice, an act of love that comes with a cost. It costs my son something to care for his sister more than he cares for his own will. He isn't always good at it. But when he is faithful to giving himself away in love, our little corner of Granger, Indiana, reflects the divine love of the Word made flesh. Not bad for a five year old.

The remembering of Christ's gift of love to the world, the art of sacrifice, makes the family aware of its vocation as a place of communion for the world. Through day-to-day sacrifice, through living out the love of Christ, the family learns the art of eucharistic solidarity. In Catholic social teaching, solidarity is the virtue of recognizing the humanity and human need of each and every other human being. According to the *Compendium of the Social Doctrine of the Church*, solidarity in the family

> can take on the features of service and attention to those who live in poverty and need, to orphans, the handicapped, the sick, the elderly, to those who are in mourning, to those with doubts, to those who live in loneliness or who have been abandoned. It is a solidarity that opens itself to acceptance, to guardianship, to adoption; it is able to bring every situation of distress to the attention of institutions so that . . . they can intervene.[17]

Such solidarity always makes me think about my grandmother, who loved her husband, her daughter, and her grandchildren. She would do anything for us—and she often did. And I was never surprised to see my grandmother stop in a grocery store to buy food for someone. She was friendliest to those in most need and was sometimes taken advantage of by those who recognized this in her. She was not stupid, but rather, she was holy. It was from her, as well as from my parents, grandfather, and brother, that I learned to care for those who are most in need. It is from my children that I have learned to care for my students, to consider not only their grades but their well-being. Family life promotes communion with each and every person.

Thus, the family really is the domestic church. It is a privileged space of communion that is deepened through regular participation in the eucharistic sacrifice. The memory of love revealed in husband and wife is incarnate in children. The sacrifice of love made present in the Eucharist is lived out in day-to-day life. And all human beings are drawn into the drama of this love as the family moves beyond its own boundaries to share divine life with the world. It is for this reason that Cardinal Ouellet writes, "In these first years of the third Christian millennium, a new missionary spirit and a true missiological orientation should have the family as its catalyst and great promoter."[18] The Christian family is the privileged catalyst for the New Evangelization.

Conclusion

Through the Sacrament of Marriage, husband and wife become signs of Christ and the Church; their love is meant to become divine. And in the reception of Christ's Body and Blood at Mass, they become what they receive: a sacrifice of love given to the world.

Remember in chapter 1 that the hookup culture has at its roots a fear of communion. Men and women hookup because they're afraid of what it would mean to enter into total, self-giving love. Such fear is natural. It's hard to love unto the end, to make oneself vulnerable to rejection.

The healing of the hookup culture, thus, can't just be about getting people to have the right kind of sex. Instead, it's about renewing a longing for the right kind of communion. The family, formed from the communion of husband and wife, may be more helpful here than we realize in this renewal.

For the family is the space where we learn to really commune with one another. It's not always especially easy. Families suffer from poverty, violence, bad parents, adultery, and more. But the communion established in family life can't just be erased. You can't just run away.

If the communion of the family was established through our own efforts, it would fail. But in the domestic Church, we discover that communion is always first and foremost a gift from God. We learn that in order to love our husband or wife, our brother or sister, and our grandfather or grandmother, we need a source of communion that's not just self-created. We need a love that comes from God.

The healing of hookup culture is thus easier than we imagine. It starts in families where genuine communion is fostered from the very beginning. Families that commune first and foremost at the eucharistic altar of God.

Exercises

1. Living out the eucharistic mystery of the Church is the heart of married life. With your boyfriend or girlfriend, fiancé(e), or spouse, read a copy of *Bored Again Catholic: How the Mass Could Save Your Life*. Complete together some of the practices at the end of each chapter. Then reflect together on why the Mass is important for your dating life, your engagement, or your marriage.

2. Share together your own experiences of remembering God's love, practicing sacrifice, and learning communion in family

life. Discuss how you want your own family, whether future or present, to live out the eucharistic mystery.

3. Marriage is oriented toward eternal life, teaching us to see what union with God is like. Where in your life of love have you discovered a bit of heaven? What does this teach you about the love of God that you will enjoy in eternity?

4. **For Marriage Formation:** Marriage formation must take the Eucharist seriously. How might you start to form engaged couples, as well as long-married couples, in their eucharistic vocation? How could you teach couples, even before they have families, to practice remembering, sacrifice, and communion?

6.

A Letter to Young Adults

Note: This chapter is a letter written to the many young adults I've taught about the healing possibilities of the Sacrament of Marriage. While this letter serves as a formal conclusion to the book, for many young people reading this book, it would be "right and just" to begin here.

Dear Reader,

Obviously, you're interested in love. Who isn't? From the time we awaken to the possibility of romantic love, we find ourselves involved in the "love lives" of our friends. We want to know their love interests. We end up talking to each other about what we long for in a boyfriend or girlfriend. As we get older, we start speaking about marriage. What would it be like to be married? How will I know I'm ready to give myself to another person forever? Will I ever be ready?

We also know that it's not always easy to find love. Many of us have learned this the hard way. We have entered into relationships where our beloveds were more interested in themselves than in our happiness. They used us to feel good about themselves. They saw us as a prize that they could brag about to their friends. They loved being around us but were unwilling to commit to being there during difficult times. They used us for our bodies, for the pleasure they experienced in the sexual act. And the hardest part is that we often do not discover that we are not really loved until it's too late—until our hearts are broken.

Despite the wounds that love can often bring, we are nonetheless made for love. We are made for communion. That's the story the Church wants to tell about men and women. But you undoubtedly know that there is another story out there that contradicts the Church's. At a young age, your friends, boyfriend, or girlfriend asked you when you hoped to lose your virginity. You felt the pressure of having or initiating sex early in a relationship because it was the norm. You heard on TV or in movies that sex usually happens on the second, third, or fourth date (at the latest). And when you entered the world of young adults, you noticed that hooking up (whatever one means by that) was separated from what you really longed for—love. It was a sloppy, drunken, easy-to-forget physical encounter with someone whose name you vaguely knew. It was not what you hoped for during those heady conversations with your friends about the nature of love. You didn't expect to have sex with someone in the hope that they might want to enter into a relationship with you, only to discover that they now avoid you whenever they can. You didn't expect the sorrow that came along with this decision to have sex. You were told, after all, that uncommitted sex was just a normal thing that people do when they're young.

Now, some of you see this movement toward uncommitted sex (or whatever you mean by hooking up) as a good thing.

Hooking up is just the normal way men and women relate to each other. It's just the new dating. You think the Church needs to get with the times and follow along. Since sexual activity is going to happen (we can presume), we should make it safe. The Church should encourage conversations about consent, emphasize the use of contraception in hookup situations, and help young men and women deal with the emotional turmoil that comes with this new order. Stop being so conservative, you say, and adjust to the modern age.

But the problem of the modern age is that it often forgets the value of the person. The Church believes that the physical act of the hookup can't be separated from the rest of what it means to be a human being. The Church is aware that what we do with our bodies forms our memories, our intellect, our understanding, and our will. The Church knows, from years of experience of working with young people, that if we engage in uncommitted sex, we are formed in a habit of non-commitment. We are formed to think that sex and love—physical pleasure and communion—are separate from each other. We'll seek out the pleasure of sex, forgetting that the union of man and woman is intended for something much greater. This union is intended not only for pleasure, but for a real sharing of our lives (including our identity as sexual creatures) with another person and for the procreation of children. We are made for communion, for the deepest friendship possible between a man and a woman.

The Church's understanding of marriage as a sacrament holds up this vision of man and woman as destined for communion with each other and with God. Too often we interpret the Church's teaching on marriage as opening the door to sanctioned sex. In other words many people think that once you're married, you can have sex as often as you'd like. Even good Catholics fall into this error, expecting married sex to function as a quasi-sacrament. This is probably the worst way of understanding the Sacrament of Marriage, because it suffers from the same narrowness that exists among those hooking up. It reduces love to sex, just as hooking up does.

On the contrary, in the Sacrament of Marriage, the loving communion between man and woman is consecrated to God. The exchange of vows, a sign of a mutual surrender of wills, is strengthened by the power of the Holy Spirit. Yes, we are made for love, but we are limited creatures. We grow tired of one another. We can't imagine what it would mean to be with our spouse as they suffer through cancer, as they deal with depression, as they undergo a midlife crisis. Yet the sacrament ensures that this natural love, this natural communion between man and woman, will last. This means that our relationship will be oriented toward love, a total gift of self, first and foremost. Sex too will be oriented first toward a total gift of oneself rather than being oriented first toward pleasure.

In marriage, sex has a new meaning. It is not first about personal pleasure, although it is of course pleasurable. Sex is not the be all and end all of romantic love. Sex is an aspect of love which is oriented toward communion. Sex is likewise oriented toward the birth of children—toward the sharing of love with the whole human family until death do us part. Couples who have been married for a long time know this. They know that the most marvelous part of marriage isn't the sanctioning of sex but the fruits of the love that blossoms between husband and wife. They know that their married love is what enables them to love their children and their friends or carry out careers that in various ways, big and small, change the world.

In the Catholic worldview, the goal of marriage, thus, is not the sanctioning of mind-blowing sex. There is a naïveté in placing sex at the center of marriage. That spouses have vowed their lives to one another doesn't mean that sex is now without the potential for harm. Husbands and wives can still use sex as a way of controlling one another. Marriage, after all, does not free people from sin. Instead, marriage elevates the communion of man and woman, giving it a new horizon: the love of Christ and the Church. This love is best understood as God's desire to be in communion with the human family. It is a love in which the Church learns to offer her own will to God. It is a divine love.

Divine love is a lot to expect from a couple. After all, we're human and not God. But the wonder of marriage, especially one oriented toward communion, is that we don't have to learn to love in this way immediately. Married couples in the Church attend the celebration of the Mass weekly, receiving the total love of God through eating and drinking Christ's Body and Blood. This practice (just like the hookup culture) shapes our memories, our desires, and our wills. Our receiving of divine love is what ultimately enables us to love our spouse in a divine way.

Such divine communion takes practice. It means remaining patient with our spouse when they leave their socks on the floor (it also means not leaving your socks on the floor . . .). It means finding time for husband and wife to share what they're thinking about. It means having children (if possible), teaching these children to pray, and in the process discovering a new openness to prayer within ourselves. It means recognizing that the gift of love between husband and wife is intended to be shared with those in need: the widow, the orphan, the lonely, the despairing.

You can see, hopefully, that sacramental marriage is much richer than the sanctioning of sex. It's a particular form of communion between man and woman that becomes a way of mediating divine love to the world. The love I receive from my spouse, a love that has been transformed through the love of Christ and the Church, is now the love I offer to my children, to my students, and to every person who needs it.

As it turns out, we are interested in love. We are interested in love because we are made for a communion that we cannot even imagine: eternal life with God. This is what the Sacrament of Marriage promises for us. It promises a love that is greater than a single orgasmic moment in which we lose ourselves in the embrace of another. Love promises communion. And sacramental marriage can allow this communion to flourish. Marriage heals us, giving us a new story by which we can live out our lives: God is love, and we are made for this love.

Appendix:

Marriage Formation in a Hookup World

While presenting on the material in this book, I have often faced this question from catechists and pastors: What program for marriage formation works best in a hookup culture? The answer I give: none. This isn't because the programs that exist are terrible. They aren't. Rather, it's because proper formation for marriage cannot be delivered by a program intended to make engaged couples ready for marriage. Formation for the Sacrament of Marriage extends well beyond the period of engagement. It ought to begin when a child is born into a family and end with death. It is an education into love. This insight is pivotal to the vision that Pope Francis lays out in chapter 6 of his apostolic exhortation *The Joy of Love.* Renewing lifelong marriage formation in the Church requires not a program but a commitment to theological education, missionary formation of families, better seminary education, forming of a sacramental imagination in Catholic pastoral counselors and family thera-pists, and promotion of spiritual direction for married couples.

For these reasons, rather than offer a comprehensive pro-gram for marriage preparation, I want to present six guidelines for developing marriage formation in a hookup world:

1. Teach cultural analysis
2. Contemplate love
3. Emphasize dating and spiritual direction
4. Present the nuptial kerygma
5. Practice consent
6. Form the domestic church

I have chosen six guidelines because six is considered an incom-plete number within Christian theology. You, the reader, can and should happily add your own.

1. Teach Cultural Analysis

The Church has a responsibility to teach young people to ana-lyze hookup culture. It is not enough to condemn this culture or to warn of the dangers of pornography. We have to teach people to think about the cultural liturgy of hooking up.

Such teaching ought to start earlier rather than later, and at home. It should expose children to the assumptions undergirding hookup culture, including understanding sex primarily as an occasion for pleasure, the fear of communication and intimacy, and the reluctance to commit. Parents as well as parish and Catholic school personnel should teach children to critically "read" the subtle stories told by the media about the nature of love—the presumption behind movies, magazines, books, and news articles of the normativity of the hookup culture. These are hard conversations to have. But the very act of talking to kids about these things is part of the medicine for the hookup culture. Children, even teens, are constantly learning from their parents patterns of behavior that shape how they see the world.

Teaching analysis is not enough. It's one thing to know the good; it's another to do it. We need to reconsider the practices by which we form our young people. Children should not be given untethered access to the Internet at a young age. Denying your child a smartphone may be a fight you would rather avoid. But by doing so you may help him or her to sidestep pornography, as well as the habit of thinking of human beings as avatars rather than persons.

Likewise, we have to teach the practice of dating. For instance, make sure that you actually leave your car and greet your date at the door instead of texting them, "I'm here." And we can explain how to ask a good question on a date that shows you're actually interested in getting to know the person in front of you.

The important thing in this education is to be direct. Even very young children will ask questions about sex and love and marriage. We ought to respond to what they ask in language and detail appropriate to their ages. As they mature, talk to children *directly* about pornography. Talk to them *directly* about the problems of hooking up. Look them in the eye. Walk with them through the media they consume, showing what it does. I've learned working with my undergraduates that they don't always agree with me, but they appreciate being taken seriously.

Colleges and universities, of course, need to perform their own cultural analysis and reform of practices. My suggestion would be for Catholic campus ministries, as well as residence hall systems at Catholic schools, to develop a curriculum that teaches about communion rather than sex. Student affairs professionals will address the legal requirements of sexual education. They'll deal with the act of sexual consent, and they might even talk about what "good" consent would look like. But, at present, they're not focusing on hookup culture as a cultural liturgy. And they're not teaching a Catholic account of love and sexuality grounded in marriage and family life. Perhaps, such campus ministries and residence hall communities would find it beneficial to require a book like *Off the Hook* for all first-year students as a way of starting the conversation. Discussions around this book should be led by faculty, ministers, and other staff who are themselves married. Students will begin to see new possibilities for love and communion not simply through reading the book but in the presence of witnesses who have themselves experienced healing through marriage.

2. Contemplate Love

Philosophy has always been part of Catholic education. Today, philosophy is nearly absent from high schools, youth groups, and even colleges. Young people are formed to think about love in ways that are detrimental to their flourishing, especially in a hookup culture. If love is simply a matter of passion, then there is nothing objective to it. One should feel free to pursue one's desire however one wants to.

Good philosophy is essential in Catholic education. I don't mean that students need to be given a history of major philosophical ideas from Plato to Immanuel Kant (although that would be fun for a few nerds like myself). Instead, I mean that they should be introduced to philosophy as a way of learning to be reasonable, to look at reality as it exists (rather than as what we think it is). A philosophical education into love should form us to see love as more than passion or desire. We should see love for what it is: communion.

There is a rich tradition of Catholic thinking about love that extends back hundreds of years before St. John Paul II's *Theology of the Body*. St. Paul, St. Augustine, St. Bernard of Clairvaux, St.

Hildegard of Bingen, St. Thomas Aquinas—they all thought and wrote about love. Further, reflections on love are universally available in philosophy and literature, film and painting, drama and poetry. Young people need to be exposed to as much of this material on love as possible.

Thinking about love won't change the hookup culture per se; we need new practices. But if our understanding of love is devoid of a sense of reason as looking at the real, then our young (and probably we ourselves) will continue to equate love with passion or sexual desire rather than with communion.

3. Emphasize Dating and Spiritual Direction

Hookup culture eschews dating. Dating involves communication. It involves directness. It aims toward sharing a life with one's partner, not just having sex with them.

We have a responsibility to re-create dating cultures in schools, homes, and parishes. We should reintroduce the practice of dating not as hooking up but as a way of getting to know someone who could be one's beloved. This means we need to lay out for young people a *regula*, or rule, for dating. I tell my students that if they want to take someone out for a date, they should ask them face-to-face. They should pay. They should go to a place where it's possible to have a conversation. They should avoid immediate physical intimacy. They shouldn't be drunk. Once they're a couple, they should talk about marriage early on. They should do things together that they'd want to do as married couples: exercise together or attend concerts, lectures, or sporting events.

And all along, they should be talking with a spiritual director or mentor. The problem with love is that we can lie to ourselves about it. In learning to love another person, we discover some of our own worst faults. Through having someone they can use as a mirror, who will ask difficult questions, young people may be able to relearn dating practices that eventually kill hookup culture. It's possible that they will receive the human formation that makes them less likely to look at pornography or to reduce their beloved to an object. And maybe more of them will come to celebrate the Sacrament of Marriage.

4. Present the Nuptial Kerygma

Christian marriage takes up natural love and makes it supernatural. It takes a natural good (communion between a man and a woman) and allows it to become a mirror of a divine good (the communion of God with the human race). If we want young people, as well as couples long married, to see their vocation in this light, they need to know how God's love has entered into history.

When I travel to parishes or schools, I find that precious few really know what it means to say that Jesus Christ is the Bridegroom. It seems no one quite grasps what it means to say that the Church is the Bride. These images have been forgotten or rejected from our Tradition, in part because they could be abused if they are understood as saying that the husband is in control and the wife is not. At more conservative colleges, I've heard it claimed that women should not enter careers or get a college education because husbands are "heads" of the household and women just need to stay at home and "submit"! This is bad theology, a poor reading of the scriptures, and just plain nonsense.

But just because an aspect of the Tradition can be misunderstood doesn't mean that it should be eliminated. Closer attention to the nuptial image of the communion of love of Christ and the Church shows us that marriage is not about the struggle for power but is instead about self-giving love. Both husband and wife submit to Christ first! Only then, healed of the desire to grasp for control, can they give their wills to one another.

We need scriptural catechesis for young people that teaches them this nuptial imagery early in adolescence. As they grow older, they should receive a deeper theological education into the Sacrament of Marriage as a contemplation of this imagery. Adults in parish life should discover in such imagery a chance for theological reflection, looking at their own lives in light of what has been revealed in Christ. They should be able to tell their own stories as icons of Christ's love for the Church. They should learn from mystics of the Church such as St. John of the Cross how human love forms us for divine love and vice versa.

Homilies in particular have a role to play here. During the liturgical year, we regularly hear readings about God's nuptial love for Israel, about Christ's love for the Church. Homilists should preach on these texts. They should interpret liturgical seasons in light of their nuptial themes. Bishops, priests, and deacons need to talk about marriage more often, not just when they're teaching about sex. In Advent, we await the coming of the Bridegroom. In Christmas, we celebrate in the Incarnation the wedding between heaven and earth. In Lent, we thirst for the living God, desiring to give our full selves away at Easter. Easter is the wedding feast of the Lamb. In Ordinary Time, we contemplate the kingdom of God. Each of these seasons presents an opportunity to invite everyone in the parish to think anew about the nature of their marriages through an encounter with the Good News that God loves us as a bridegroom loves his bride.

5. Practice Consent

The Sacrament of Marriage requires more than learning the story. It involves entering into the drama of practicing consent. Consent, for baptized Catholics, creates a permanent bond between the man and woman. Their love is now Christ's love. Christ's love is their love. This means that Catholic married couples need to practice this love in their day-to-day lives and thus become central figures in the formation for marriage of younger members of the Church. This is true for not only their own children, but all to whom their enduring consent becomes a witness of love.

At a natural level, this simply means that spouses should continue to romance and to take care of each other. Bring little gifts home regularly. Put the kids to bed when it isn't your turn. Return text messages immediately instead of waiting until the end of the day. Call when you're going to be late. Take your husband or wife out on a date. Practice caring for one another.

At a deeper level, this means taking one's religious life seriously. Couples sometimes wait too long to consider what prayer practices they might build into their lives. Once they get married, they pray only when they're together. This is bad news! If the couple is going to reflect the love of Christ and the Church, then they must learn to contemplate this love as individuals. Each spouse needs to develop a personal order of prayer in which they learn to delight regularly in divine love. For some, it will be eucharistic adoration. For others, listening to Catholic music in the car. It could be the Rosary or the Liturgy of the Hours. Whatever it is, the prayer approach needs to permeate one's life.

In addition, the couple should practice loving those who are most in need of love: the hungry, the thirsty, the lonely, and the sorrowing. Catholic marriage formation should provide a basic introduction to Catholic social teaching. Learning to practice mercy will make it easier to be merciful to one's spouse and children, to love as Christ loved the Church.

Older couples should see it as their duty to oppose the hookup culture by outwardly witnessing to the sacramental bond of their marriages. Ideally with the help of parish structures, they can mentor adolescents and young adults about what to look for in a spouse. They should share their stories. They should invite young people into their homes for dinner, letting them help put the kids to bed. Elderly couples should be given opportunities in parish settings to share their wisdom about love. Perhaps it would be good to link up members of the youth group with widows or widowers who could provide insight about the art of self-giving love.

In each case, the practice of authentic consent would be fostered. That is, younger couples would see that consent in marriage is really about sticking together through good times and bad. Consent is learning to see how every part of our love story is slowly transformed as we spend day after day with our spouse becoming an image of Christ's love to the Church for another and for our children. We need to tell such stories in our parishes and schools regularly.

6. Form the Domestic Church

There is nothing more important to the New Evangelization than the formation of the domestic church. Marriage formation, from the beginning, should highlight the vocation to family life that is the orientation of nuptial love. At an early meeting for immediate marriage preparation, couples might receive the basics for a home altar or prayer corner: icons of Christ and the Blessed Virgin Mary, a Bible, a candle, and an adapted version of the Liturgy of the Hours for daily use along with simple coaching about how to utilize these things. This may seem extreme, as we do want to meet people where they're at, but a material gift is precisely what many young people want. They know that falling in love is a big deal; it awakens in them a sense that they want God to be part of this relationship. Giving concrete objects and a form through which the couple can learn to pray together is really quite helpful if not essential. Of course, a parish representative must introduce the home altar or practice of prayer in a way that teaches the couple and explains why it is important. A young couple who perhaps had been suspicious of this gift but learned how to use it might serve as an important witness. In addition, when and if the couple is blessed with children, the parish should send another icon, perhaps linked to the child's patron saint.

Both parents and children should be engaged in regular theological reflection about the nature of their life together. They should learn to look for God's presence in spousal love, in fraternal care, in the mundane aspects of daily life. Groups in parishes should be gathered together often to reflect on God's presence in the family. The family should be given concrete practices to perform at home—the less complicated, the better. Yes, family catechesis is key, but this catechesis often unfolds in the home as moms and dads celebrate seasons and feasts with their children.

Families also need help to become a place of hospitality. Whole families should be encouraged to come regularly to funerals in the parish, assisting in burying the dead. They should be persuaded to welcome refugees, immigrants, all those who are in need of Christ's own hospitality. Missionary formation in parishes shouldn't be limited to training individual disciples to spread the Good News. The whole family should be viewed as an agent for evangelization.

Younger adolescents and young adults then become medicine for the hookup culture by living within it without partaking in it, articulately sharing why they don't engage. They can share the wisdom of the Church's vision of love with those who don't know it. They can offer an alternative story, an alternative vision. Cultures can be changed. All that is needed is a subculture strong enough (and strategic enough) to drive the transformation.

Conclusion

Franz Biebl's "Ave Maria" echoed through the Basilica of the Sacred Heart as Kara and I knelt before a statue of the Blessed Virgin Mary. Before we found each other, we had loved others. We had had other dramas, other stories that formed our imaginations. Yet just moments prior, we had promised fidelity to each other for the rest of our lives. We had taken up a new story, a new set of practices, that would forever change our lives. We were now contemplating our Blessed Mother's words, asking that they be made our own: "May it be done to me according to your word" (Lk 1:38).

Every marriage should begin as demonstrating this openness to God's will that was expressed so perfectly by Mary, the Mother of God. In this sense, we could think about every moment of marriage formation as helping husband and wife to take on a bit of this Marian character.

Like Mary herself, this gift of our will to God will not always be easy. It's often really hard to love our spouse in the same way that Christ loved the Church. It's very often difficult to raise kids to know how beautiful self-sacrifice is. It's hard when our spouse may be diagnosed with a terminal illness, one that requires us to say goodbye, to let them enter into life with God without us. Real communion, true love, is always hard. The hookup culture, of course, brings challenges that may be unique to our age. But marriage formation has always been really hard for us fallen men and women.

But it was hard for Mary too, and we have her as our model and advocate. In fact, we have a cloud of witnesses to intercede for us before the triune God. We're not alone. The Queen of All Saints and her husband, St. Joseph, knew the mystery of married love. They knew what it was like to promise to love one another until death. They knew what it was like to raise a child together, to wash him, to feed him, and to care for him when he was sick. They shared in the total mystery of married life, in friendship and companionship, for as long as St. Joseph lived. And Mary endured watching her husband and son die.

Mary intercedes for us not just on our wedding day but for the rest of our lives. For, like her, we are consecrated through the nuptial mystery to let the Word made flesh transform every dimension of our love.

Mary, Mother of God, Wife of St. Joseph, pray for us.

Exercises

1. Read through the above guidelines for marriage formation. How would you concretely implement these in your parish, school, or home?
2. What would you add to this list of guidelines?

Notes

Introduction

1. Mark Regnerus, *Cheap Sex: The Transformation of Men, Marriage, and Monogamy* (New York: Oxford University Press, 2017), 97.

2. Donna Freitas, *The End of Sex: How Hookup Culture Is Leaving a Generation Unhappy, Sexually Unfulfilled, and Confused about Intimacy* (New York: Basic Books, 2013), 34.

3. Freitas, 188.

4. Center for Applied Research in the Apostolate, "Frequently Requested Church Statistics," accessed October 24, 2017, http://cara.georgetown.edu/frequently-requested-church-statistics/.

5. Sofia Cavalletti, *The Religious Potential of the Child: Experiencing Scripture and Liturgy with Young Children* (Chicago: Liturgy Training Publications, 1992), 172.

6. James K. A. Smith, *Desiring the Kingdom: Worship, Worldview, and Cultural Formation* (Grand Rapids, MI: Baker Academic, 2009), 25.

7. Freitas, *The End of Sex*, 182.

8. Francis, Post-Synodal Apostolic Exhortation *Amoris Laetitia (The Joy of Love)* (Vatican City: Libreria Editrice Vaticana,

2015), https://w2.vatican.va/content/dam/francesco/pdf/apost_exhortations/documents/papa-francesco_esortazione-ap_20160319_amoris-laetitia_en.pdf, 71.

9. Jean Corbon, *The Wellspring of Worship*, trans. Matthew J. O'Connell (San Francisco: Ignatius Press, 2005), 117.

10. Timothy P. O'Malley, *Liturgy and the New Evangelization: Practicing the Art of Self-Giving Love* (Collegeville, MN: Liturgical Press, 2014), 31.

1. Hookup Culture

1. Freitas, *The End of Sex*, 25.

2. Freitas, 29.

3. Mark Regnerus and Jeremy Uecker, *Premarital Sex in America: How Young Americans Meet, Mate, and Think about Marriage* (New York: Oxford University Press, 2011), 56.

4. Regnerus, *Cheap Sex*, 82.

5. Matt Rosoff, "Ashley Madison Was a Bunch of Dudes Talking to Each Other, Data Analysis Suggests," *Business Insider*, August 26, 2015, http://www.businessinsider.com/ashley-madison-almost-no-women-2015-8.

6. Caitlin Flanagan, *Girl Land* (New York: Little, Brown, 2012), Kindle e-book, chap. 2.

7. Regnerus, *Cheap Sex*, 35.

8. Regnerus and Uecker, *Premarital Sex in America*, 25.

9. Regnerus, *Cheap Sex*, 99.

10. Nancy Jo Sales, "Tinder and the Dawn of the 'Dating Apocalypse,'" *Vanity Fair*, September 2015, https://www.vanityfair.com/culture/2015/08/tinder-hook-up-culture-end-of-dating.

11. Regnerus, *Cheap Sex*, 69.

12. You may find this survey online at: http://relationshipsinamerica.com/ (accessed May 5, 2018).

13. Regnerus, *Cheap Sex*, 115.

14. Pamela Paul, *Pornified: How Pornography Is Transforming Our Lives, Our Relationships, and Our Families* (New York: Times Books, 2006), 17.

15. Gail Dines, *Pornland: How Porn Has Hijacked Our Sexuality* (Boston: Beacon Press, 2010), 102–103.

16. Regnerus and Uecker, *Premarital Sex in America*, 98.

17. Regnerus, *Cheap Sex*, 165.

18. Although an older book in need of some revision, Michael Kimmel's *Guyland: The Perilous World Where Boys Become Men—Understanding the Critical Years between 16 and 26*, 2nd ed. (New York: Harper Perennial, 2009) documents the increased "adolescence" of men in particular.

19. Regnerus, *Cheap Sex*, 205.

2. Love as Communion

1. Karol Wojtyla, *Love and Responsibility*, trans. Grzegorz Ignatik (Boston: Pauline Books, 2013), 96.

2. Unknown, "Lyric 23" in "Poems of Adoration" in *Medieval English Verse*, trans. Brian Stone (New York: Penguin, 1964; repr. 1986), 57.

3. Karol Wojtyla, "Thomistic Personalism," in *Person and Community: Selected Essays*, trans. Theresa Sandok (New York: Peter Lang, 2008), 173.

4. Dietrich von Hildebrand, *Marriage: The Mystery of Faithful Love* (Manchester, NH: Sophia Institute Press, 1991), 12–13.

5. Wojtyla, *Love and Responsibility*, 121.

6. Von Hildebrand, *Marriage*, 21–22.

7. Wojtyla, *Love and Responsibility*, 156.

8. Wojtyla, *Love and Responsibility*, 257.

9. Jessica Keating, "Celibacy at 30 Is Not Just an Empty Holding Pattern," *America* magazine, September 18, 2016,

https://www.americamagazine.org/faith/2016/09/08/
celibacy-30-not-just-empty-holding-pattern.

3. Love's New Story

1. Joseph Ratzinger, *Collected Works,* vol. 2, *Theology of the Liturgy: The Sacramental Foundation of Christian Existence* (San Francisco: Ignatius Press, 2014), 163.

2. English translation of *The Order of Celebrating Matrimony,* 2013, International Commission on English in the Liturgy, no. 52.

3. Bernard of Clairvaux, *On the Song of Songs,* vol. 1, trans. Kilian Walsh (Kalamazoo, MI: Cistercian Publications, 1971), III.6.

4. Readings for the Sacrament of Marriage can be found here: http://www.foryourmarriage.org/catholic-marriage/planning-a-catholic-wedding/readings/. You could also consult Joseph Champlin and Peter Jarret, *Together for Life,* revised with *The Order of Celebrating Matrimony* (Notre Dame, IN: Ave Maria Press, 2016).

5. John Paul II, *The Theology of the Body: Human Love in the Divine Plan* (Boston: Pauline Books, 1997), 76.

6. Benedict XVI, *Encyclical Letter Deus Caritas Est (God Is Love)* (Vatican City: Libreria Editrice Vaticana, 2005), http://w2.vatican.va/content/benedict-xvi/en/encyclicals/documents/hf_ben-xvi_enc_20051225_deus-caritas-est.html, 17.

7. John Paul II, *Theology of the Body,* 312.

4. Be Mine

1. *The Order of Celebrating Matrimony,* no. 62.

2. *The Order of Celebrating Matrimony,* no. 2.

3. Matthias Scheeben, *The Mysteries of Christianity*, trans. Cyril Vollert (New York: Herder and Herder, 2008), 584.

4. Scheeben, 604–605.

5. Marc Ouellet, *Mystery and Sacrament of Love: A Theology of Marriage and the Family for the New Evangelization*, trans. Michelle K. Boras and Adrian J. Walker (Grand Rapids, MI: Eerdmans, 2015), 80–81.

6. *The Order of Celebrating Matrimony*, no. 64.

7. *The Order of Celebrating Matrimony*, no. 62.

8. Dietrich von Hildebrand, *Transformation in Christ: On the Christian Attitude* (San Francisco: Ignatius Press, 2001), 456.

9. Karol Wojtyla, *The Jeweler's Shop: A Meditation on the Sacrament of Matrimony, Passing on Occasion into a Drama*, trans. Boleslaw Taborski (1980; repr., San Francisco: Ignatius Press, 1992), 33–34.

10. *The Order of Celebrating Matrimony*, no. 67A.

11. *The Order of Celebrating Matrimony*, no. 67B.

12. John S. Grabowski, *Sex and Virtue: An Introduction to Sexual Ethics* (Washington, DC: Catholic University of America Press, 2003), 46.

13. *The Order of Celebrating Matrimony*, no. 68.

5. Lift Up Your Hearts

1. Hildegard of Bingen, *Scivias*, trans. Columba Hart and Jane Bishop (New York: Paulist Press, 1990), II.6.1.

2. *The Order of Celebrating Matrimony*, no. 200.

3. Adrienne von Speyr, *The Holy Mass*, trans. Helena M. Saward (San Francisco: Ignatius Press, 1999), 80–81.

4. Timothy P. O'Malley, "Waiting for Gabriel: Learning to Pray through Infertility," *America* magazine, October 22, 2012, https://www.americamagazine.org/faith/2012/10/22/waiting-gabriel-learning-pray-through-infertility.

5. Paul Turner, *Inseparable Love: A Commentary on the Order of Celebrating Matrimony in the Catholic Church* (Collegeville, MN: Liturgical Press, 2017), 140.

6. *The Order of Celebrating Matrimony*, no. 207.

7. *The Order of Celebrating Matrimony*, no. 207.

8. Francis, *Amoris Laetitia*, 181.

9. *The Order of Celebrating Matrimony*, no. 207.

10. Francis, *Amoris Laetitia*, 166.

11. See Susan Windley-Daoust, *The Gift of Birth: Discerning God's Presence during Childbirth* (Winona, MN: Gracewatch Media, 2016).

12. Timothy P. O'Malley, "A Trinitarian Love: The Sacramentality of Adoption," *America* magazine, September 23, 2013, https://www.americamagazine.org/issue/trinitarian-love.

13. Gabriel Marcel, "Creative Vow as Essence of Fatherhood," in *Homo Viator: Introduction to a Metaphysics of Hope*, trans. Emma Craufurd (New York: Harper & Row, 1962), 124.

14. *The Order of Celebrating Matrimony*, no. 207.

15. John Paul II, Apostolic Exhortation *Familiaris Consortio (On the Role of the Christian Family in the Modern World)* (Vatican City: Libreria Editrice Vaticana, 1981), http://w2.vatican.va/content/john-paul-ii/en/apost_exhortations/documents/hf_jp-ii_exh_19811122_familiaris-consortio.html, 17.

16. Anna Keating, "The Perfect Family Is an Idol," *Church Life*, October 2, 2017, https://churchlife.nd.edu/2017/10/02/the-perfect-family-is-an-idol/.

17. Pontifical Council for Justice and Peace, *Compendium of the Social Doctrine of the Church* (Vatican City: Libreria Editrice Vatican, 2004), http://www.vatican.va/roman_curia/pontifical_councils/justpeace/documents/rc_pc_justpeace_doc_20060526_compendio-dott-soc_en.html, 246.

18. Marc Ouellet, *Divine Likeness: Toward a Trinitarian Anthropology of the Family*, trans. Philip Milligan and Linda M. Cicone (Grand Rapids, MI: Eerdmans, 2006), 76.

Timothy P. O'Malley is a Catholic theologian, author, speaker, and managing director of the McGrath Institute for Church Life at the University of Notre Dame. He is an associate professional specialist in the Department of Theology at Notre Dame, also serving as academic director of Notre Dame's Center for Liturgy.

O'Malley earned his bachelor's degree in theology and philosophy and his master's degree in liturgical studies from Notre Dame. He earned a doctorate in theology and education at Boston College.

He is the author of three books, including *Bored Again Catholic* and *Liturgy and the New Evangelization*. His articles have appeared in publications including *America* magazine, Religion News Service, *Aleteia*, *Catechist*, and *Our Sunday Visitor Newsweekly*.

He lives with his family in the South Bend, Indiana area.